IN PRAISE

IN THIS BOOK, TONY WHITEHEAD has written about people that he knows, and the choices they make in their lives Tony has many insights from his time in law enforcement, but he also writes from his heart. He has the love of Christ in his heart for other people, and he has experienced the grace that is available to all people in Jesus Christ. He knows about the things he speaks. There's not a lot written these days about what becomes of people who turn their back on God. Tony looks into the lives of people he grew up with, people from his hometown, and people whose story would not be known if Tony had not written it for us. While no one but Jesus Christ can be the final judge of another person, Tony has witnessed the destructive lifestyles and poor choices of others he has known. It is not a judgement, but a reminder of the mistakes that any of us can make, and what can happen when we do.

All people are important, and all lives matter, especially to God It is in this spirit that I believe Tony offers his insights into the pain and loss many families suffer when they allow self and sin to rule their lives. If people weren't important to Tony, he would not have written this book.

I appreciate this book as a wake-up call, and also a help to the people of today's generations. Some who read this may be on the same kind of path as those they will read about. I think that's the point.

So, I give thanks to God for all people of faith who, like Tony, see to share the truth to God and the truth of the coming judgement. Let those who have ears to hear, listen. Then choose to follow Jesus.

Pastor W.B. Burch

IN *LETTERS FROM HELL*, Tony Whitehead has done a memorable job of challenging people to ponder one's future.

Our society pursues instant gratification, God calls us to view our identity through the lens of His Word. Tony takes an

Intriguing and personal look at the eternal consequences of our decisions. Whether you are a Biblical scholar, or new to the faith, *Letters from Hell* will both challenge and inspire.

Dr. Joe McKechnie, Pastor
Mountain View United Methodist Church

I beg you to read these stories carefully. Open your heart to the Holy Spirit. ... Try to understand the depth of regret [n the letters].

Dr. Roberta Wallace

LETTERS FROM HELL

LETTERS OF WASTED LIVES

TONY WHITEHEAD

NOTE FROM THE PUBLISHER

Blank pages within this book are intentional.

The author intended this book to be read with prayer and contemplation and to be used as a reference and a study guide. Therefore, it contains pages intentionally left blank on which the reader can write down thoughts and notes.

TABLE OF CONTENTS

FORWARD

I AM BOTH HUMBLED AND excited at the same time. I am humbled by the privilege of introducing this material. I am very excited at the prospect of the reader seeing something from a different angle never before seen by that reader.

The author Loves the Word of God, and the burden of his heart is the desire to bring Christian brothers' and sisters' truths from God's word that will challenge them and encourage them to dig even deeper into the Bible. The main result will be a closer relationship with Jesus as Savior and Lord of their life. Thus, with excitement, my prayer for you is that as you read this book written by Tony Whitehead, you will grow to love the Savior more and have a deeper passion for the Word of God than you have ever experienced before.

There are two themes that consistently run thru the Bible. They are the family and home, and eternity – Heaven or hell.

God had created man in His own image. God had given man a mind to be able to understand God. A heart that would love God and a will that would be in tune with the will of God. God gave to man a woman that man might be complete, and thru their union, a race would be born; a race that would have the mind, heart, and will of God. God's plan was right and perfect. It was

Man, who failed. Everyone knows the story of the fall.

Let it be known that the enemy, the Devil, cannot touch the home where a man and a woman are of one flesh, where both of them are committed to God's will and are living by the authority of the word of God.

The second theme that runs thru out the Bible is the theme of heaven and Hell or eternity.

Where is it that most people get their information about Heaven and hell? Most people develop their ideas of both Heaven and Hell from the arts: Painters, Musicians, Film, and Poetry. There is a popular theory that because God loves the whole world, He will change His nature to embrace the hope that all will go to Heaven. But Malachi 3:6 tells us that God does not change and that God has prepared Heaven for those that believe and obey God.

Those who repent of sin receive God's forgiveness, and God sees that person as covered and seen through the righteousness of Jesus. Those that repent go to Heaven, those that refuse God go to Hell. It is a choice; it is your choice. Jesus spoke more about hell than He did about Heaven.

Hell has been disguised in fiction for so long that people deny the reality of such a place. It is time for the Church to declare to all believers the full counsel of God. God declares in His word how to get to Heaven and how to avoid hell. Hell was created for the Devil and his demons. Satan wants to take the entire world with Him.

Charles Spurgeon writes: "Meet me in Heaven. Do not go down to Hell. There is no coming back from that abode of misery. Why do you wish to enter the way of death when Heaven's Gate is open before you? Do not hesitate and delay. Again,

I charge you. Meet me in Heaven." —Charles H. Spurgeon, taken from *All of Gracie*, Copyright 1983, Whitaker House

It is my prayer that these words written here have created a deep desire within the reader to study the Word of God in a more serious way than ever before. Don't read books about the Bible. Read the Bible itself.

Our author, Tony Whitehead, has included 17 letters written from Hell to loved ones hoping that they might change their course in life before it is eternally too late.

I beg you to read these stories carefully. Open your heart to the Holy Spirit. Read each story slowly. Try to feel the pain of these people residing in Hell. Try to understand the depth of their regrets. But it is now too late for them! They said no to Jesus.

What about You?

It is not too late,

Jesus, the son of God, sent to Pay the Price

For our sin, to become Savior and Lord over all

And give us the promise of Heaven.

Dr. Roberta Wallace
June 2020

INTRODUCTION

A FEW YEARS AGO, MY FATHER sent me an early rough draft of "Letters from Hell." This draft did not have the number of 'letters' that are in this publication; however, it was enough that I was caught up in the message that is prevalent throughout this book. That message points to our need for a Savior. That Savior IS Jesus Christ. There is no other way around it. On this matter, Christ said, "I am the Way, and the Truth, and the Life. No one comes to the Father but through Me."

What you will find in these pages will grab you and force you to consider your eternity. Where will you go? The better question is, "Have you accepted Christ as your Savior?" Have you surrendered to Him? Simply believing in Him won't help you. You have to accept Him as your Savior. You have to repent, and you have to surrender.

What you will find in these pages are the fictitious stories of people who didn't do any of those things. They lived their lives for themselves and for the world. It's what we find today. Many people are all about themselves with little concern for anyone else. The evidence? The evidence of God's love isn't in their hearts. They live for worldly things and not heavenly things.

Therefore, having read through this book several times, I will tell the reader that this is one of the most thought-provoking publications that I have read next to the Bible in some time. The stories will grab you, and yes, they will force you to consider our shared commonality, which is the mortality of our bodies and the immortality of our souls. I am forever amazed at what God does through people who allow Him to work through them. I'm proud of you, Pop!

Pastor Nolen Whitehead
Center Terrace Baptist Church
Canton, MS

PREFACE

WHAT EXACTLY MOTIVATED me to write this book—*Letters from Hell* ?

A while back, I began thinking over the many years of my life and the various people I had encountered along the way. First as an auxiliary deputy sheriff in a large Alabama city, then the 48 years I spent covering the entire southeast as a salesman, and finally as a neighbor and friend to many. I began wondering what had become of these people. Many of these people were from my school days as far back as the 5th grade. They came from all walks of life. Most passed away many years ago due to the choices they made and the lifestyles they lived.

The Bible tells us not to judge our fellow man, lest we be judged. Only God can judge the hearts of people. All of these stories and circumstances are true. The only part that is fiction is their descent into hell and their responses once there. We can only speculate what someone might experience and what their response might be. I do not think that the finite human mind can comprehend what awaits us on the other side of death, whether in Heaven or hell. The Bible probably gives us more insight into the horrors of hell than it does the glories of Heaven. I have included an entire chapter devoted to what the Bible says about hell (printed with permission from the KJV Dake Annotated Reference Bible) from Genesis to Revelation. There is only one account we have of a taking place with anyone in hell, and it is in the parable of *Lazarus and the Rich Man* found in Luke 16:19-31, as told by Jesus himself.

Secondly, someone may pick up a copy of this book, read it, and says to him or herself, "I am just like the person in that story. Why it's almost as if this was written about me." If upon personal reflection, that person sees the need to make changes in their life and accept Jesus Christ as their Lord and Savior, then this book will have accomplished its purpose. If, by some chance, a reader sees the direction their children, spouse, brother, or sister is going and can use any of this material to help win them to Christ, then I will have accomplished what I set out to do.

> *"Except the Lord build the house, they labor in vain*
> *that build it:*
> *Vs. 3 - Lo, children are a heritage of the Lord: and the*
> *fruit of the womb is his reward." Psalm 127: 1 & 3*

Let us look at a modern-day (hypothetical, of course) family of Dad, Mom, Jr., and little Susie. Mom and Dad are both in high paying stressful jobs, with the children spending most of their time in daycare and later in private schools. We will examine a typical week beginning on Monday morning.

Dad gets up at 5:00 am to shower, dress, and get to the airport by 8:00 am for a flight out of town that will keep him away till late Thursday night. In the meantime, Mom arises at 6:00 am, showers, and gets dressed by 6:30 am. She gets Jr. and Susie up for breakfast consisting of a bowl of cold cereal. The children are strapped in their car seats by 8:00 am and dropped off at daycare by 8:30 am Monday through Friday. Each day at 5:30 pm, she picks up her two little angels, goes home, and fixes them a somewhat nourishing meal or calls out for a pizza more often than not. No later than 8:00 pm, the children are in bed.

Dad gets home about 10:00 pm on Thursday and sticks his head in the door to "check on the kids." Friday afternoon, Dad picks up the kids promptly at 5:00 pm and goes to the pizza parlor, where Mom joins them by 5:30 pm.

Mom has now spent 25 hours with her children since Monday morning. Remember, the children must be in bed by 8:00 pm, so dad has spent a grand total of 3 hours with his most precious (?) possessions. Saturday morning comes, and Dad is up at 7:00 am to meet his buddies at the golf course for a 9:15 T-time. He plays golf and has lunch until 2:00 pm. He comes home by 2:30 pm to spend some time with his beloved children. In the meantime, on Saturday morning, Mom gets the kids up at 8:00 am for another bowl of cold cereal and pop-tarts. She then has a teenager from across the street come over to babysit at about 9:00 am so she can meet up with an old college girl-friend, go shopping, and have lunch. She arrives back home at about 3:00 pm. Then Mom and Dad leave the kids with a babysitter at 6:30 pm and head to the country club for dinner and dancing until after midnight. Again, the kids are in bed by 8:00 pm.

Sunday morning is slightly different because Dad has a hangover from too much partying the night before, so he stays in bed until 11:00 am. Of course, he is in a foul mood when he does get up, but he makes the best of it and spends a total of 9 hours with the children today. Mom does a little better. She lets the kids sleep until 9:00 before getting them up for pop tarts and a bowl of oatmeal; after all, it is Sunday. She spends a total of 11 hours with her children today.

Look at the totals for the week:

Mom – 40.5 hours for the week out of 168 hours

Dad – 16.0 hours for the week out of 168 hour

Of course, this is a hypothetical scenario. But is it? How many families in the United States are raising their children in this fashion? It almost seems normal today. How many stay-at-home moms or dads do we have today? How many do you know? I know of three.

One of the many problems with an affluent society like ours is that we must "keep up with the Joneses" down the street. In our modern society, Dad must work long hours and spend much time traveling all over the country or world to make big money. Because of lust for bigger and nicer things and because Mom has just as prestigious a degree as Dad, she must also work long hours to pay the bills and buy trinkets. In their minds, they have no choice but to park their most precious possessions in a childcare facility week after week and year after year. Then comes vacation time, and it is off to a resort somewhere that has a golf course for Dad and a spa for Mom. The children, well, they are dropped off at Grandma's with no thought of taking them along.

Is it any wonder that children growing up in this manner rebel against their parents when they become teenagers? Can you wonder why some turn to alcohol, drugs, or sex? They have felt no real love at home and instead have looked to friends for a little affection and understanding. Seeing how some parents shirk their God-given duty of raising their children to know Jesus and accept him as their personal Savior, I suppose it is a little too much to expect. But too many of today's parents do not know the Lord themselves. Understandably, they keep reaching out for more achievements or more things, never quite finding what they are seeking after. Greed has taken control of their lives, and they do not even realize it. They are like a rider on a carousel trying to catch the brass ring to win the prize, but it is always just out of reach.

Too many of today's parents have rejected their duty as parents to raise their children in the fear of the Lord, and that makes them abject failures as parents. However, if someone were to ask them point-blank, "how are you doing as parents," their answers would revolve around all the latest gadgets and toys they had bought for their children. Unfortunately, today's parents think that the more things cost and the more things they give to their children, the better off they will all be. Of course, friends and neighbors will see that Mom and Dad buy only the most expensive and best things for their offspring. What wonderful parents they must be!

I hope that many parents will read this introduction, continue on to read the letters enclosed within these pages, and see a little of themselves in them. Maybe they will see the disaster they are creating for their offspring and will seek the Lord as their Savior, encouraging their children to do the same. I do not think there is any man or woman alive that would say, "I want my son or daughter to go to hell," but that is precisely what too many of us are doing in today's world.

May God forgive us,
Tony Whitehead

HPOTHETICAL FAMILY-QUESTIONS

1. How do you compare yourself to
   the Mother_____
   the Father_____

2. WHAT CHANGES IN YOUR LIFE DO YOU NEED TO MAKE?

   1. the Mother_____
   2. the Father_____

   3. How much importance does each of you put on material things?

   1. the Mother_____
   2. the Father_____

4. Is "KEEPING UP WITH THE JONES'S" MORE IMPORTANT THAN YOUR children?

the   Mother_____

the Father_____

5. HAVE YOU ACCEPTED JESUS AS YOUR SAVIOR?

the Mother_____

THE FATHER_____

6. IF YOU ANSWERED "NO" TO THE QUESTION ABOVE, WILL YOU now decide for Christ for the sake of your children?

1. the Mother_____

2. the Father_____

BIBLICAL FOUNDATION

THE ACTUAL EXPERIENCE of two beggars: the contrast of their lives on earth and their experience in death.

The story is a literal one of two beggars. One begged for food in this life; the other begged for mercy in the next life. This parable in the book of Luke shows plainly the conditions of departed souls between death and resurrection.

> "19 <u>There was</u> a certain rich man, which was clothed
> in purple and fine linen, and fared sumptuously
> every day:
> 20 And <u>there was</u> a certain beggar named Lazarus,
> which was laid at his gate, full of sores,
> 21 And desiring to be fed with the crumbs which fell
> from the rich man's table: moreover, the dogs came
> and licked his sores.
> 22 And it came to pass, that <u>the beggar died</u>, and was
> carried by the angels into Abraham's bosom: <u>the</u>
> <u>rich man also died and was buried.</u>

23 *And in hell he lifts his eyes, being in torments, and
seeth Abraham afar off and Lazarus in his bosom.*

24 *And he cried and said, Father Abraham have mercy
on me, and send Lazarus that he may dip the tip of
his finger in water and cool my tongue for I am
tormented in this flame.*

25 *But Abraham said, Son, remember that thou in thy
lifetime receivedst thy good things, and likewise
Lazarus evil things: but now he is comforted, and
thou art tormented.*

26 *And beside all this, between us and you there is a
great gulf fixed: so that they which would pass from
hence to you cannot; neither can they pass to us
that would come from thence.*

27. *Then he said, I pray thee therefore, father, that thou
wouldest send him to my father's house:*

28 *For I have five brethren; that he may testify unto
them lest they also come into this place of torment.*

29 *Abraham saith unto him, they have Moses and the
prophets; let them hear them.*

30 *And he said, Nay, Father Abraham, but if one went
unto them from the dead, they would repent.*

31 *And he said unto him if they hear not Moses and
the prophets, neither will they be persuaded, though
one rose from the dead." Luke 16:19 - 31*

FACTS ABOUT LAZARUS (LUKE 16:22)

1. He was a beggar full of sores which the dogs licked (v 20-22).

2. He laid at the rich man's gate to beg the crumbs from his table
(v 21).

3. He died and his body was buried (v 22).

4

4. Angels carried his soul and spirit to paradise (v 22).

5. He was with Abraham and all the redeemed (v 23).

6. He was in comfort: no hell, no torment, and no separation from the saved, no crying for mercy, no regrets of the past, and no thirst or punishment in hell's fire (v 24-26).

Facts about the rich man (Luke 16:22)

1. He was clothed in purple and fared sumptuously every day (v 19).

2. He died and his body was buried (v 22).

3. His soul went to hell (v 23).

4. He was in torment (v 23-25, 28).

5. He possessed eyes that could see and distinguish persons (v 23).

6. He cried for mercy and begged for Lazarus to bring a drop of water to cool his tongue (v 24).

7. He still had a tongue, eyes, memory, intelligence, feelings, emotions, will, voice, reasoning-powers, concern for his brothers, and

all other soul passions and spirit faculties (v 23-31).

Compare yourself to the two people described in the BIBLICAL FOUNDATION:

1. Which person best describes you?

a. the HusbandLazarus _____The rich man _____

b. the Wife - Lazarus _____ The rich man _____

2. What changes in your life do you need to make to enjoy the fruits of salvation like Lazarus?

the   Wife

_____

the Husband _____

PURPOSE

LETTERS FROM CHILDREN IN HELL TO
THEIR PARENTS:

WITH THE HOLY SPIRIT'S HELP and guidance, I will attempt to write this as if it were a child addressing a letter to his/her parents asking a simple question. Also, I will try to write in a simple language style that might be spoken by a person in torment. Incidentally, the writer of this letter may be teenage, middle-aged, or old age.

The one thing that I sincerely hope to accomplish is that some of you parents and future parents will see yourselves in some of these letters, realizing that you need to make changes in your lives for the sake of your children. Or, just as important, you may see someone you know or work with that fits the same description as some of these people. You may be able to give them this little book and hopefully bring them to Christ. Perhaps as you read, you will relate to some of the character flaws in these people, i.e., greed, selfishness, lack of moral principles, and in some cases, plain old-fashioned idolatry. We have many idols in our society today, not just the graven images spoken of in the Bible. We have movie stars, rock stars, rap stars, football players/teams, baseball players/teams, and probably the most insidious of all – the pursuit of the almighty dollar. In modern society, we have put wealth above everything, including God and our families, to the extent that many families are torn apart or barely exist as a unit because of greed. How many modern-day families sit down at the table for breakfast, lunch, or dinner?

For the most part, it is said our children will grow up in our footsteps, especially when raised in a kind, loving and Godly home. It is almost a universal understanding that when a child grows up in a broken or abusive home, they will, at a minimum, have many psychological problems. The chances are high that their own homes will be abusive or broken later in life as well. Some will never be able to retain a stable relationship with a spouse. They will just drift from marriage to marriage, always blaming the other person when the actual foundation of their failure can be laid on you, their parent. One of the big problems we all face is taking responsibility for our own actions, whether that problem is with our marriage, our children, at work, or accepting or rejecting Jesus Christ as our Savior. Remember that being indifferent to Christ is the same as rejecting Him.

The letters in this thin volume are based on real experiences with people in my personal life. I cannot assume whether any of these people are in Heaven or hell. None of us can know the answer to that question about someone else. We can only assume a given outcome of their life after death based on their lifestyle while alive. Some of these people may have repented of their sins and asked Jesus Christ to save them. I certainly hope so. We must remember at Christ's crucifixion, one of the thieves on a cross next to him made a simple statement. Luke 23:42-43 says, "And he said unto Jesus, Lord, remember me when thou comest into thy kingdom. And Jesus said unto him,

"Verily I say unto thee, today thou shalt be with me in paradise."

The poor fellow didn't even have time to be baptized.

Every one of the people in the following letters had an opportunity to come to Jesus for salvation. People do have a conscience but refuse to accept what it is telling them and instead depend on their own intellect and selfish ways.

NOTES FROM THE AUTHOR

LOOKING BACK OVER more years than I care to count, I have seen a steady decline in true Bible-believing churches with many preaching false doctrines now more than ever. 2 Timothy 4:3-4 tells us:

> *"For the time will come when they will not endure*
> *sound doctrine; but after their own lusts shall they*
> *heap to themselves teachers having itching ears;*
> *and they shall turn away their ears from the truth,*
> *and shall be turned unto fables."*

Lies rule the day. We are truly in the times where Scripture warns us, "everyone is doing what is right in their own eyes." This is my paraphrase of a comment by Ronald Reagan, "it is not that we are uninformed, ...but that we are misinformed. So much of what we believe simply is not true."

In our lifetime, we have seen the Supreme Court outlaw prayer and Bible reading in schools. Abortion on demand has become legal to the tune of many millions of unborn children murdered for the simple reason that a baby would be inconvenient and unwanted. Prayer is no longer allowed at sporting events on public school properties or in some courtrooms and town hall meetings.

However, it is my opinion that the Muslim Koran is tolerated in these public arenas where the Bible is not. This creates familiarity with other religious doctrines that many in the Christian world consider to be dangerously opposed to the Biblical teachings of Christ.

Thanks to a decline of morality in our schools, there has been a steady falling away from the "things of God." Today our inner cities are practically war zones with rape and murder. Drugs of every sort imaginable are constantly available.

The time has come for us to realize that we must turn back to God if we are to survive as a nation. He will not let us go much further down the slippery slope that we are on. We have turned our back on him and, in a sense, told him to go away and leave us alone. Our current situation cannot and will not last forever. As a people, we worship too many idols, i.e., baseball, football, basketball, alcohol, pornography, vile music, and the almighty dollar.

Many parents today have abandoned their children because they simply do not want to be bothered, so they are left to survive the best way they can. Thus, gangs proliferate even in affluent neighborhoods.

It is time for parents to stop thinking only of themselves. Whether or not they believe in God and the Bible, it is time to start thinking of the enormous responsibility with which each parent has been entrusted. I believe a child is born innocent and remains unaccountable until they reach an age of accountability. Although this may be a different age for each one, it usually occurs around 8 to 12 years old when a child learns the difference between right and wrong. As a child gets older in truth, it becomes increasingly more difficult for them to turn to Christ, so by the time they have gone through college, there is little hope for them becoming a Christian, or at least it is much harder for them to accept Christ. It is a parent's duty, honor, and privilege to raise their children to know Christ as their Savior. If they do not, they are failures as parents. I don't care how much material success they may have; they are still an abject failure as parents.

I have heard several people make these statements. "Jesus and the Bible is all just a fable and not worth giving up your desires and carnal lifestyle." "All these phony preachers are just out for money and living a high life." "I just don't believe anything these preachers claim is true; they are just a bunch of liars."

I knew one very successful used car dealer in Baton Rouge, LA, that I invited to go to a Billy Graham Crusade at the LSU football stadium in 1971. This man went on a tirade, cursing me for asking him and cursing Billy Graham. He claimed that Billy Graham spends more every month on "whores and whiskey" than he made in a year. He went on with his tirade against Billy Graham, churches, and then cursed God. I watched this man over the next few months and years. Within six months, he was broke and went from selling one to two-year-old extremely nice cars to selling junk for $400/$500 and barely making a living. With his continued cursing God and all things holy, his health began to fail, and he became a pariah among local car dealers. He finally went out of business.

You may not believe anything that the Bible teaches. You may scoff at everything holy and reject God. That is your choice. When God created man, he gave him free will, which means we have the ability and intellect to obey and worship him or to ignore him.

> *"And this is the will of him that sent me, that everyone that seeth the Son, and believeth on him, may have everlasting life: and I will raise him up at the last day." John 6:40*

I would rather live in obedience to God's word. I believe in Jesus Christ and am His child. I believe that when I die, I will be His in Heaven immediately. I choose to live according to Biblical teachings and have a much more rewarding life now and in the hereafter. If, when I die, I find there is no Heaven or hell, I will still have lived a far better and more rewarding life than I would have had by living a life of sin and disregard for all that is holy and good.

For a moment, think about this. You have married. You and your wife now have several small children. You are determined not to lead them to a saving knowledge of Christ because you don't believe or care. Why should they?

You and your wife live to old age, and both of you die within a few years of each other. You are instantly in hell in intense torment and torture. You have now learned that everything that you rejected your entire life was true. The fire burns continuously. It never stops day after day. There is no such thing as escape from hell, and now you can see that you were absolutely wrong for all those years.

Time goes by for a few years, and then your son is suddenly with you in this place of torment. He blames and curses you for not teaching him about Jesus. He entirely blames you for his predicament. Next, your daughter comes to join you, your wife, and your son. Looking ahead, all your grandchildren will one day join you because of your unbelief. Despite your mother and father's pleas, you rejected everything holy and are now paying the ultimate price. You have destroyed your descendants forever. Probably their best hope is that they are lucky enough to marry a God-fearing spouse who will lead them to Christ.

WORKNOTES

QUESTIONS TO BE ANSWERED about the Purpose and Notes from the Author:

1. How many idols* do you have in your life? (List them below)

a. _____ b. _____

c. _____ d. _____

e. _____ f. _____

2. Do you and your family attend Church on a regular basis?
_____ yes _____ no

3. Are you raising your children (or children to be) to love and honor God as their personal Savior?
_____ yes _____ no

4. How many times in a fit of anger, have you told someone to

"go to Hell?" _____

5. I don't know of any parent that would tell their child or children to "go to hell," but if they are raising them absent of any teaching about Jesus Christ, then that is exactly what they are telling them. What is your position on this all-important question?

_____

_____

6. We have taught our children, or children we may have in the future, to believe in Jesus as their Savior and to love and worship him all the days of their lives.

_____ yes _____ no

*An idol can be almost anything that you place your time and energy into, i.e., sports, work, movies, pornography, a hobby that takes up an inordinate amount of your time.

PART I

THE LETTERS

LETTER 1

ALL AMERICAN FAMILY

"TRAIN UP A CHILD in the way he should go: and
when he is old, he will not depart from it."
Proverbs 22:6

Mother,

I thought we were a perfect example of a Christian family. What is happening to me? I vaguely remember going to work this morning at the bank. I have been working for a member of our church in his bank as a loan officer and part-time teller. It was great until this morning. I remember someone wearing a Halloween mask pointing a gun at me and demanding money. The last thing I remember was a loud bang and me falling. I kept falling and falling until I finally landed. There were flames everywhere, but nothing burned up. I was on fire, and I didn't understand why. There are millions, no billions, and billions of people here, and all of them are crying, screaming and cursing, begging, and pleading for relief. Mother, this place is worse and more frightening than any Steven King book or horror movie. I think that I must be in the hell that we always heard about and never really believed existed. This place is more horrible than the human mind can understand.

Why am I here? We went to church every Sunday. You were in charge of the Women's Fellowship and taught Girl's Sunday School class for years. You carried me to church when I was in the nursery, and I continued to attend through high school. I admit that I did slack off a little while in college because Sunday was the only day that I could sleep a little late. As soon as I returned from college and got married to my high school sweetheart, we were right back in church every Sunday and most Wednesday nights. Mom, you were one of the pillars of our little church, and everyone looked up to you. You raised my younger sister and me right by the Bible. You never spared the rod because discipline was paramount to you, and we learned from an early age to be respectful and to obey our elders

Then there was Dad. He was the head deacon for many years and was always the head of the Finance Committee. He usually taught Intermediate Boys Sunday School classes. I remember Dad always saying a blessing before eating any meal, even when we were in a restaurant—always! Dad had a daily devotional just after we finished dinner. It was usually short but straight from the church's daily devotional booklet.

When my sister came along, she was the pianist for the Youth Department at Church. Everyone thought she was a beautiful young lady, always so prim and proper. She was a favorite at church and president of the after-school Bible Study Club.

We did have an idyllic life growing up. Sis and I never wanted for anything. However, we did learn to work at an early age. She was a volunteer in the local hospital. I volunteered at the local animal shelter and worked on Saturdays at a pet store. When we went off to college, Dad was able to pay our way through without either of us having to take out any student loans. We were so blessed.

As I look back over my life and church life now, I vaguely remember our preacher giving something he called "an altar call" occasionally. I never really understood what it meant, so I always just remained in my seat. I didn't want to make a spectacle of myself like I saw some of my friends do, crying in front of the whole congregation. You asked me one time when I was going to join the church. My answer to you was that I thought I was automatically a member since you and Dad were members and because I was christened in the main sanctuary at about two months old. You didn't try to argue with or correct me, so that subject never came up again. I thought that I was a member in good standing. Besides, Dad told me that it wasn't necessary for me to "make a confession of my faith" before the congregation. He never had, and said, "just look at me; I'm as good a Christian as anyone here."

I remember my third year in college when Dad passed away from a massive heart attack, and the church rolled out the red carpet for his funeral. Everyone who came through the receiving line kept telling us that, yes, it is hard to give up such a wonderful husband and father but not to worry because sooner than we could think, we would all be joined again in Heaven.

I believed them and always knew that we would be together with Dad in Heaven until a few moments ago.

I saw Dad! He is here just like me and tormented with everlasting fire and sores. I thought we were the ideal Christian family. What went wrong, what happened? Someone came up to me and told me that the reason Dad and I are here in this horrible place is that neither of us had ever accepted Jesus Christ as our Savior. We had never asked or invited Him into our hearts or repented of our sins. We had just coasted along and learned to say the right things to impress a lot of other church members who were coasting along as well.

After being in this wretched place for some time now, I have come to realize that other people did have a major Christian impact on my life. Still, I chose to reject every opportunity to repent and accept Jesus' salvation. Mom, I really can't put all the blame on you for my eternal predicament. I had many chances as a youth growing up and as an adult, but I rejected every opportunity just like Dad.

If you could only receive this letter written to you from the depths of hell, I would admonish you; no, I would beg you to seek and find Christ as your personal Savior and encourage Sis to do the same. Whatever you do, do not end up in this horrid, putrid place with Dad and me. Please remember Jesus' words in John 3:18

> "He that believeth on him is not condemned: but he
> that believeth not is condemned already because he
> hath not believed in the name of the only begotten
> Son of God."

Like so many people, I had a hard time believing John 3:16, and that is why I am here now. It is your problem too. I suppose we had all heard of Jesus our entire lives, but because of our unbelief in John 3:16, which says,

> "For God so loved the world, that he gave his only
> begotten Son, that whosoever believeth in him
> should not perish, but have everlasting life."

I just didn't believe these words. In my mind, how could a loving God create such a place as hell?

QUESTIONS

1. ALL AMERICAN oFAMILY

1. How does your family compare to the "All American Family"?

    a. about the same _____ yes _____ no

    b. Completely different _____ yes _____ no

2. As a family, do you have daily devotions? _____ yes _____ no

3. Do you as a parent encourage your children to learn and participate in Church activities?

    a. the Mother _____ yes _____ no

    b. the Father _____ yes _____ no

4. Do you as a parent set an example for your children by participating in Church activities?

    a. the Mother _____ yes _____ no

    b. the Father _____ yes _____ no

5. Are you a "born again" Christian?

    a. the Mother _____ yes _____ no

b. b. the Father _____ yes _____ no

6. Have you encouraged your children to accept Jesus as their personal savior?
    a. the Mother _____ yes _____ no
    b. b. the Father _____ yes _____ no

7. If your answer is no; then why not?

a. the Mother _____

b. b. the Father _____

LETTER 2

WILD CHILD

ABOUT 40 YEARS AGO, A FAMILY built a new house across the street from where I lived. It was the largest house in the entire neighborhood, and it was evident that the father was doing very well for himself and his family. There were two daughters, high school and college-age, and one son about twelve years old when they moved into the neighborhood. Over time, we became friends with the parents, and I observed many things about the young son. He was rebellious toward his parents and any authority figure, and he had a hard time getting along with other kids. This boy was an extreme risk-taker when playing with the neighborhood kids. One might say that he was a daredevil and many of his attempts at showing off for the other kids backfired.

One such instance was with the BMX bicycles. The kids had stacked some boards and made a ramp to jump with their bicycles. It wasn't too dangerous at first because it was only about a foot high and situated on the lawn. If a boy and his bike fell, at least he landed on some thick grass, and chances of injury were slight.

This wasn't good enough for Billy (not his real name). Billy moved the ramp over onto the concrete sidewalk and raised it well over two feet. He then backed his bike farther down the street and pedaled as fast as he could. As Billy hit the ramp and went airborne, he came down hard and fell over to his left side. He was lucky this first time and only had a few scrapes and bruises.

He was not done, however. He moved his bike farther down the sidewalk so that he could get up more speed. This time, he went over the handlebars and landed hard on the concrete breaking his left arm and fracturing his right wrist.

Now any reasonable person would have learned a lesson from this accident, but not Billy. He was back on the sidewalk a few days later, trying the same trick again. This time he ended up with a concussion and several broken ribs. His dad took the bicycle away from him and donated it to Goodwill.

When the Smiths (not their real name) first moved into the neighborhood, they went to a large Methodist church and were stalwart members. Every Sunday morning, I would see them as a family leaving for Sunday school and church services. Something happened along the way because, by the time Billy was in high school, he rarely went to church with his parents except on special occasions.

In all the years that I knew this family, I never heard any of the adults or the two daughters use any kind of curse words or vulgar language of any sort. Not true of Billy. He was a paragon of virtue around his mother, father, and sisters, but around the other kids, he was as foul-mouthed as the proverbial drunken sailor, totally disgusting. He was becoming such a blow-hard and braggart that my two sons stopped associating with him altogether, as did most of the other neighborhood kids.

Billy's mother would come over to our house just to talk and get away from her son. She would break down crying because they could not seem to get through to him. He wouldn't listen to anything she or his grandparents would say to try to get him to straighten his life up. She knew he was drinking and suspected him of using drugs because of some of the unsavory new friends he was associating with. It was about this time during the summer before his freshman year in college that he had his first run-in with the law. He was drunk, ran a red light, and clipped the back end of a car that had the right of way. He was arrested for driving under the influence. The wreck was entirely his fault, and his insurance wouldn't pay damages because he was drunk. His dad paid for repairs on the other people's cars. What happened to Billy's car? His dad bought him a new pick-up truck with a much more powerful motor.

According to Billy's mother, the problem was that her husband practically worshiped "little Billy" as he called him. He believed anything and everything that Billy told him. Nothing was ever Billy's fault, and he was intelligent enough to get decent grades in school without studying more than a bare minimum. Billy got into many scrapes while in high school because of his bad behavior.

One example she told us was when Billy and some of his friends spray-painted some racial epithets on a restroom wall on the last day of school. Billy's dad had to pay to have the entire boys' locker room, and restroom painted to keep "Little Billy" from getting expelled from school for the next year.

Did Billy's dad punish him for this act? No, because Billy told his dad that he just happened to be in the restroom when these other boys did the deed and that he didn't have anything to do with it.

Billy's poor mother was at her wits' end as to what to do about her son and his father. With tears streaming down her cheeks, she told us tale after tale of the different things Billy had done or gotten into in the last few years of high school. It was unbelievable that his father couldn't or wouldn't see the destructive path his son was on. She made the statement that afternoon, about three weeks before college classes were to begin that it would be amazing if he made it through four years of college without killing himself or someone else. How prophetic.

In the meantime, Billy's father had started his own company, refurbishing and selling rather expensive medical equipment worldwide. He had been in this business for over 30 years and had a great client base already built up. He started out doing very well for himself, and it seemed as though the more money he made, the more he doted on his wayward son.

As neighbors, we watched from afar, just waiting for the disaster to happen. And happen it did. Billy had pledged a fraternity and had been to a party at the frat house. There had been a lot of drinking, and some "pot" passed around till the wee hours of the morning. Billy and a fraternity friend got in Billy's pick-up and headed home. The road leaving campus ran by a series of lakes and was very curvy, with a lot of old oak trees on either side.

Billy started out driving very fast, even though it had been raining and was still sprinkling. He always drove very fast and did not fasten his seat belt. His friend asked him to slow down several times, but Billy, the show-off, speeded up as usual. His friend asked him about his seat belt, and Billy's answered that he never wore one because they were for sissies. About this time, Billy hit a large puddle of water in the middle of the road and lost control of the pick-up. They went down an embankment and slammed into a large oak tree.

Billy was thrown from the vehicle and into another one of the trees. He was killed instantly. His friend? Well, his friend escaped with a few cuts from broken glass and a broken ankle, but he survived. The state trooper investigating the accident said that Billy would have survived if he had been wearing his seat belt.

From birth to his death, Billy had every opportunity to know the Lord and live a full and productive life, but he chose not to.

At first, He couldn't understand what was happening. He was on fire but was not consumed. He thought maybe his truck was on fire, and somehow, he was trapped. He then began to look around and see all these other people in the same predicament. He began to realize where he was but could not understand why until much later.

Then something strange happened. Billy was floating near a ceiling in a large room filled with people. There was a strange quietness about this place, with only an organ softly playing. Then everyone in the room stood up, and there was Mother, Daddy, his two sisters, and both sets of grandparents, along with a lot of aunts and uncles, all walking down the center aisle. Making their way to the front of the room, they stopped by this strangely decorated box that was surrounded by huge arrangements of flowers. Finally, he was able to look down into the box.

No, it couldn't be, but it was. It is was him! He looked all pale and stiff. His hair was perfectly combed, and everything looked artificial.

Then, He looked at his dad. He had never seen him cry in all his life, but he was crying uncontrollably, almost like a small baby that was stuck with a diaper pin. He shouted out to him, "Daddy, please stop crying," but he didn't hear. He shouted louder, but nothing. Then there were his mother and his sisters crying, and his grandparents as well.

~

In Billy's words:

At first, I had difficulty understanding what was happening to me, but I kept looking back into that strange box, and I didn't move. I listened intently as the preacher and several other people spoke about me and what had been my life. What did they mean by, "What had been my life"? I still didn't understand what was happening; I had never been to a funeral before, so I had no clue until they closed the lid on that strange box.

Somehow, I followed that box outside to a strange SUV looking vehicle. Many cars lined up behind them, and they drove a few miles to a large field with a lot of marble markers standing upright all around. They carried the strange box over to a large hole in the ground and said some more kind words about me. Mother, Daddy, and my sisters were crying uncontrollably as they began lowering the box into that hole in the ground. I shouted and kept shouting, "please don't put me in the ground like that." Now I was crying uncontrollably. I looked around, and all the people had gone. The workmen were dumping dirt upon the strange box with me inside.

About this time, I awoke, and for the first time, I finally realized that I was in the depths of hell and was in torment. I now remembered what the Sunday school teachers had tried to tell me when I was a youngster about this place, that it was and is a real place. The fire was all around me; the stench was the worst thing I had ever smelled, and I realized that I would be here forever. People all around me were crying, screaming, and cursing, but we are each here because we deserved to be here. I was too stubborn and self-centered to listen to anything about the Bible, Jesus, or Christianity. I knew it all. I was a real know-it-all brat, and my best thinking brought me to this place.

~

DEAR MOTHER,

Whatever you do, please don't come to this place, and make sure that Daddy and my two sisters do not, let me repeat, do not come to this horrible place!

I know that this message from me to you can never get through to you, but somehow, I think you will just know.

Your loving son,

Billy

QUESTIONS

#2. WILD CHILD

1. Do you have a child like the one herein described?

_____ yes _____ no

2. If you answered yes, what steps have you taken to bring him/her under control?

a. _____

b. _____

c. _____

3. Assuming that your family is well off financially, have you taught your children the value of a dollar and how to work, or have you given them everything on a silver platter?

a. Taught them the value of a dollar _____ yes _____ no

b. Taught them to work for what they want _____ yes _____ no

c. Given them everything on a silver platter _____ yes _____ no

4. If your answer to question number 3-c is "yes," what areyou going to do about it?

a.

_____

b.

_____

c.

_____

LETTER 3

NEGLECTFUL PARENTS

Mom/Dad,

You always had time for your friends but never us, your children. Why? I died last night, but I doubt if you noticed. As usual, you were at some swanky country club trying to impress a bunch of other drunks. Oh, you will come to the wake and funeral and put on a great show of sadness and remorse, but it really will be phony like everything else about you. You were only interested in society and what pleasures the world had to offer. As I look back over my life growing up—to the ripe old age of 17—I can well remember all the lavish parties you and Dad threw for your fake friends. All of you are sitting around the pool drinking and smoking pot and sniffing that white powder. My sister and I watched for years at the disgusting example you set before us. I well remember when I was about 6 or 7 years old, one of our neighbors came over and invited us to go to their church, and especially for my sister and me to go to Sunday school. Mom, you told that lady that you were "not interested in that nonsense." Then you slammed the door in her face and went on a tirade about these "Bible thumpers" wanting to brainwash our innocent children and us. How sad.

I began to sneak out of the house after your parties and go out to the pool. Late one night, I found a half-smoked joint in an ashtray. I thought to myself, "why not? Mom and Dad seem to laugh and have a good time after smoking one of these. I'll give it a try." Wow! I was hooked. I was now 12, and I had a feeling that I had never experienced before. I was laughing and seemed happy. I began searching and found other pills and powders left behind because you were too wasted to clean up after yourself. I swallowed some pills and began to see all the different colors of the rainbow. I felt like I was floating on a cloud.

Very quickly, your weekend leftovers were not enough to carry me through the week. I began to search for your stash and found where you were hiding all those wonderful pills. I also found a small pipe with some funny looking little chips that looked kinda' like a broken cracker. I smoked one of those, and wow! I didn't know at the time that this was crack cocaine,

I was floating near the ceiling, looking down, and had a feeling of complete euphoria. Little did I know at the time that this was crack cocaine, one of the most addictive drugs available.

By now, I was 15 years old and hooked on drugs. All my thoughts and actions were on getting the next fix or high. I was failing in school. My appearance was slowly degenerating so that I looked more like a homeless street urchin than the son of an affluent, somewhat respectable family. I had begun skipping most of my classes a few years earlier and now seldom attended at all. The school called and tried to talk to you about my failing grades, my many absences, and my drug problem, which was apparent to everyone but you and Dad. Your response was typical for a mother or anyone with a sense of denial. You shouted and cursed the counselor and told her never to call you again, and to stop spreading rumors about her son or in the typical fashion of today's parents; you would "sue her for her last dime."

When I finally came home late that night, you were waiting up for me and told me what the school counselor had said. Of course, I denied everything in my stupor and blew it off as just an old fuddy-duddy that was just trying to cause problems for me at school. You believed me and, as usual, told me, "just be a good boy, and don't worry about it."

Mom, you and Dad were still having your wild parties every weekend but now due to my addiction your leftovers were never enough. I began stealing from the house, first from the cookie jar that always had a few dollars stashed. When that wasn't enough, I started taking things from the house to sell or trade for more pills or whatever was available on the streets. Finally, after many confrontations, you and Dad had had enough of my stealing and recognized that I was a drug addict. Dad said that when he was growing up, they had a term for people like me. They were called "dope fiends," and indeed, I fit the description. With that, I was thrown out of the house with a $100.00 bill and an admonition that if I wanted to kill myself to go ahead. At this point I realized that with your addictions, though not as severe as mine, you could not allow me to stay because seeing me would be almost like looking in a mirror of your own lives, and you couldn't face that. You couldn't face the fact that you had created the monster I had become.

~

To the Reader:

My older sister had married years earlier and moved to another state. I decided to attempt to go to her and see if she would or could help me. I had begun to realize that I had a problem and needed help.

BIG SISTER TOOK ME IN, AND I SEEMED TO CLEAN UP MY ACT FOR A short time. Her husband insisted that I go to NA (Narcotics Anonymous). That worked for a while. Then one day, while walking, a guy on a street corner offered me a hit on his joint. With that, I was off and running once again.

My brother-in-law put me out of the house. He would not put up with my addiction around their two small children. I don't blame him; he had to look out for his family.

I had just turned 17 years old and was so wasted that I forgot that it was my birthday until several days later.

I was now sleeping in abandoned buildings, under bridges, or anywhere that I passed out. Throughout the last year of my life, I was arrested several times as a vagrant, given a suspended sentence, fined, and let back on the streets.

MOM/DAD,

Finally, on the night that I died, someone came into the vacant building where several of us were staying. They gave us some new pills that were great at first, but then - MOM/DAD, I died and am in hell. You know, that place you kept telling people to go to whenever you became angry or had a disagreement. I am on fire, but nothing burns up. The stench is the worst smell that I have ever encountered. Everywhere people are screaming, hollering, and crying.

People all around me are begging for Jesus to save them.

The demons are all around us, laughing and tormenting us. They keep telling us, "call out to Jesus a little louder perhaps he doesn't hear you."

I finally realize that it is your fault I am here. You never once told me anything about Jesus or salvation or the Bible. The one time you had a chance when the neighbor lady came to the door to invite us to church and Sunday school, you slammed the door in her face and went on a tirade about the "Bible thumpers" trying to fill our heads with nonsense. I don't remember ever seeing a Bible in our house. There were plenty of drugs, alcohol, and pornography in Dad's desk drawers. Yes, you and Dad gave us every material thing we could want. But the one thing that we needed the most, you didn't give us, and that was a strong foundation in the Holy Bible and a saving knowledge of Jesus Christ. For that lack on your part, I curse you and Dad from the depths of hell. I know that my short life was a living hell because of the example you set before me, and now, thanks to you, I am here for all of eternity. Unless, by some miracle, you and Dad change your entire lifestyle and accept Jesus as your Savior, you will be joining me soon.

For once in my miserable life, I have had to stand up and take responsibility for my own actions and, yes, my own sins. I remember hearing some guy named Billy Graham saying on the radio something about, "be sure, your sins will find you out." There was a voice deep inside me, trying to tell me that I had better listen to this man because he spoke the truth. Instead, I changed the station and was miserable until I turned back to that station to catch the last few words of a song. I think it said something like, "Jesus is calling for you and for me," but the station faded out, and I didn't hear the rest, so I don't know how it ended. I know that I am here, and I had many opportunities NOT to be here, but I blew every one of them.

I know that this letter can never come to you because

"there is a great gulf between the living and the dead,
the living dead in hell and the living in heaven."
(Luke 16:26)

However, because of the misery that I see and hear all around me, I sincerely hope that you and Dad wake up and accept Jesus Christ as your Savior, and please don't end up in this awful place called hell.

QUESTIONS

3. NEGLECTFUL PARENTS

1. Looking at your family lifestyle, how do you compare to this family?
    a. the same _____ yes _____no
    b. nothing like them _____ yes _____ no

2. Are your friends more important than your own children, and do you include your children in most of your activities?
    a. the Father_____ yes _____ no
    b. the Mother _____ yes _____ no

3. Did you not realize that your children were picking up your drinking habits and using drugs at a very early age?
    a. the Mother _____ yes _____ no
    b. the Father _____ yes _____ no

4. Do you think your wild partying lifestyle influences your children?
a. the Mother _____ yes _____ no
b. the Father _____ yes _____ no

5. If you answered yes to question number 4, what do you intend to do about it and what changes are you willing to make for your children

_____

_____

_____

LETTER 4

LEGALISTIC FATHER/PASTOR

Papa/Mama,

What has happened? All that I heard was a loud crash, and now I am in this awful place. Why? I am in the worst place imaginable, and I am on fire, but I'm not burning up. I don't understand any of this. Why am I here?

There are people, or rather their spirits, all around me, in the same condition as I am, on fire but not actually burning and covered in sores. These are the most awful, scabby looking sores imaginable. Everywhere I touch myself, a new sore would popup. I am beginning to remember what happened, and Papa, it is your fault I am in this terrible place. I blame you.

You were a preacher of a rather large older church, but you were very legalistic with rules instead of preaching and teaching the love of Jesus. As a rebellious daughter, you were continually admonishing me to behave. Don't do anything to embarrass me. It was always about you. When I had problems or just wanted fatherly advice, you were away at another conference or attending to the needs of a sick church member or another meeting. You never had time for me. Why was that? I would genuinely like to know.

I can now remember growing up and having church crammed down my throat almost every minute of every day. There were four meetings on Sunday in the Baptist churches. There was Sunday school, the main 11:00 service, and another service at 6:00 pm. Then there was Training Union, and finally, the 7:30 Sunday night service that might last until 9:30 or 10:00. As I got a little older, you expected me to go with Mama to the Tuesday morning ladies Bible study meeting during the summer when school was out. I was a young teenaged girl sitting around with a bunch of old hens, bored out of my mind. Next was Wednesday night, followed by a miserable church dinner. Then Prayer Meeting that could last from 7:00 to 9:00. Finally, there was the glorious Thursday night choir practice. Most Friday nights were free except in the summer when you had something planned for the youth—which you forced me to attend. Besides all of this church nonsense, you made me wear dresses that were below my knees, something that girls might have worn back in the 1930s, and I was only allowed to wear shorts in gym class at school. Pants were out of the question. Oh, and another thing. I was not allowed to wear makeup until I was a senior in high school. However, I went behind your back. I kept my makeup kit in my locker at school and kept a bottle of vodka that one of the boys had given me.

Papa, you made my life so miserable that I rejected everything you taught and stood for. I rejected the Bible and any thought of Jesus, and I had heard plenty about him. Remembering back, I did hear a sermon by another preacher in a revival meeting about the Pharisees in Jesus' day being too legalistic. That description fits you to a "T." That was just how you raised me, but as some might say, "All of that stuff just wasn't my cup of tea, I wanted none of it." Dad, you and mom should never have had kids.

I met a guy that was a few years older than me, and we started dating. He had been on the streets for several years and knew his way around. He gave me all the beer, liquor, and sex I wanted. Yes, wonderful, glorious sex. You and Mama never told me anything about sex except that I would learn all about the "birds and bees" from my husband someday. Well, that day arrived, but he wasn't my husband. After about six months, we decided that we needed to get married before I began to show. I brought him home to meet you and Mama. You rejected him outright without giving yourselves a chance to get to know him. Later your only comments were that he was "no good," that I had better stay as far away as I could. You said you had always planned a big wedding for me with one of the nice boys from church, but you would have no part in this marriage if I chose to go through with it.

I was so upset and heartbroken that I cried for over a week and put myself in such a state that I lost the baby. That was the final straw for me. We went out of town to a small country wedding chapel that didn't ask too many questions and tied-the-knot. We were very happy for the first several months, and even though you and Mama didn't approve, you tolerated my new husband. All was bliss for a short time.

Then one afternoon, I was feeling ill, so my boss let me come home early. I went in the back door and immediately heard strange noises coming from the bedroom. I expected to open the door and catch my still new husband in bed with another woman. However, there was no woman. My husband was in bed with another man. I was utterly shocked and dumb-founded. I had only vaguely heard of these things. He came out and tried to get me to join in, but there was no way that I could take part in anything so vile and disgusting. Shortly after, his lover left, and my husband came out to talk to me. He explained in course terms that he was what some might call AC/DC, or in other words, he liked men and women and that it was no reflection on me. Out of ignorance, I stayed with him for another year or two. We would make love almost every night. Then I would go to sleep, and he would go out and find a male lover to complete his night.

Papa, about six months after I found all of this out, I came to you for advice. I told you the entire sordid filthy story of my existence. Your answer to me was that the Bible didn't condone divorce and that it was for "better or worse when we married." Your advice was, "you will just have to learn to live with things the way they are." I left your study/office for the last time that night and went to a bar and began to drown my sorrows in alcohol. Soon I was about as drunk as I had ever been when a total stranger came over and asked to buy me another drink. I thought, why not. No one else cares anything about me. I was feeling about as low as I had ever felt in my young life. This bar friend invited me to his motel room for a nightcap. I went and ended up spending the next three days with him. I know that it was not love, but it sure felt like it at the time. I went back home but could not bring myself to let the pervert I was married to touch me. Not then and not ever again.

To the Reader:

AFTER A FEW DAYS, I began to feel lonely for a man, and I remembered a used car lot where we had bought a car. They had an office and a house trailer on the backside of the lot. I remembered asking what that was for, and the owner said, "That's the adult playroom." I couldn't get there fast enough, and he was sure surprised to see me. He asked if there was anything he could do for me, and without thinking, I said that I wanted to try out the "adult playroom." He was all too accommodating, and I had a great evening with him. When the poor man was spent, I asked him if anyone else might want to play. Over the next few weeks, I spent most of my spare time in the adult playroom with who knows how many different men.

Then one afternoon, the boss man had had his way with me, and as he was leaving, he said that he had a good friend that wanted to come in. Great, I was not ready to go yet. When I heard the door open, I called out to him to get undressed in the other room because there was no place back here for his clothes. The man came in, and at first, in the dimly lit room, it was hard to see who he was. I thought, "my God, it is my uncle, Papa's brother." At first, he just acted normal, but toward the end, he said that since I was family that we should keep it in the family and that I would not be getting my usual fee. Before he left, he told me that he would be seeing me every other day and that I should just be a good girl or else.

Through all this, my husband and I had not stopped going to church. As usual, this Sunday, we were sitting about midway. Down front, a few rows sat my wonderful uncle and his family. He turned around and looked at me with an evil smirk on his face.

After the announcements, Papa stayed behind the pulpit and began to speak. He told the congregation that he must do something for the good of the church body. He needed to preserve the integrity of the youth and children of the church. With that, he looked straight at me and ordered my husband and me to stand up. Not knowing what was coming, we did as directed. Papa then went into a litany of our sins and transgressions. He told the church body everything I told him earlier about my husband being AC/DC, about how he would sleep with me and then go out looking for men. He told the congregation about my uncle finding me in the adult playroom and how much I had been charging my customers. My dear uncle had turned around in his seat and was grinning from ear to ear and said in a whisper, "gotcha."

Papa then told the congregation that he was putting us out of the church, that he could not allow his prostitute daughter and her perverted husband to remain among decent church-going folks if we were practicing our sin. I don't remember much after that. We both ran out of the church. He went one way, and I jumped in the car and began to drive rapidly down the street. Tears were flooding my eyes to the extent that I could barely see. I kept accelerating and running red light after red light until I heard a loud crash, and everything went black.

The next thing I knew, I was on fire, but it wasn't the car burning. There was screaming and crying and cursing all around me. There must be millions upon millions of people in this awful place. It has finally dawned on me that I am in a literal burning hell, and there is no escape, no way out.

Papa and Mama,

I blame you for my predicament for being so stern and rigid that you couldn't let a young girl just be a girl and grow up normally. You had to control my every move and thought. Yet look how I turned out. But, and there is always a but, I also blame myself for being here. As stern and strict as you were, just like many of the people in the Old Testament, I rebelled and brought this calamity on myself. As my eyes clear a little, I see a lot of people here that I knew while growing up, some we would never have expected to be in this awful place, this hell. I look around and see a lot of the people that we all looked up to as children, teenagers, and adults. Some were famous movie stars, rock stars, some were athletes, and some were politicians, people from all walks of life. They are all here. Oh, if I had a life to live all over again, I would change everything in my life. It is now too late for me, but you can still change so that you do not come to this awful hell. I now realize that I blamed you all my short life for all my woes, but I was really the one to blame for being the rebellious child and young woman that I became. If I only had another chance at life, I would do things totally different. I guess the old saying "hindsight" always being better than "foresight" is true.

QUESTIONS

4. LEGALISTIC FATHER/PASTOR

1. How do you compare your lifestyle to this legalistic controlling father? Do you try to control every aspect of your spouse and children's lives? _____ yes _____ no

2. If your answer is yes, what can you do to change and create a more harmonious environment to raise healthy, well-adjusted children and create peace in your marriage?

_____

_____

3. Have you ever considered that by trying to control every aspect of the lives of all the people around you that you are driving them away from you?

    a. the Father_____ yes _____ no

    b. the Mother _____ yes _____ no

4. If you answered truthfully and your answer is yes, what are you going to do to change your and your family's situation?

_____

_____

_____

LETTER 5

REBELLIOUS CHILD

THERE WAS A WELL-RESPECTED doctor in a rather large town in the South. He was a leader in his field and regarded throughout the entire country as an expert in treating burn victims. The good doctor was married to a lovely woman who did volunteer work throughout the community. They had four children, an older son followed by two daughters and a small boy to round out the family.

As was typical in this part of the South, they were devout Catholics. They supported their local parish and church both by monetary means and weekly participation in all church activities. By all accounts and appearances, this family was on solid ground for many years, Then, something happened.

Unfortunately, this same thing has happened in many families. We sometimes think that broken homes, or homes headed by an alcoholic parent, or any other number of things, are what cause dissension and split families apart. However, that was not the case here.

The oldest son began to run with the wrong crowd at school; soon, his grades dropped off. Eventually, his appearance began to deteriorate, and in a few short years, he looked like someone who had been living on the streets for a long time. He was by all accounts a pathetic specimen of what he had been.

What allowed this young man to continue in his folly? It was his father who didn't see or didn't want to see what his son had become. With the long hours he put in at the clinic and various hospitals, he had no time to notice his son until it was too late. When his mother complained about her son's circumstances, his father would usually sit him down for a long talk. The boy would straighten up his act for a while, and Dad would buy him some new toy, usually a new car, or whatever the popular fad was at the time.

A short time after the boy started the twelfth grade, he "got busted" at school, with a stash of marijuana in his car. Of course, he was arrested and expelled from school. After this episode, his parents sent him to a succession of private schools, where the same thing happened several more times. The big difference now was that Junior had gone from hoarding pot for his personal use to selling to anyone that had the money. A short time later, he learned that he could make a lot more money selling cocaine than marijuana. His parents had no idea what he was doing until one afternoon, there he was on the 5:00 news in handcuffs, being led from his wrecked car to a police cruiser. It seems that there had been an arrest warrant issued for him for selling tainted cocaine that had killed three people and sent several more to the hospital. When Junior had seen the flashing blue lights behind his car, he tried to outrun the police. That didn't work very well. He ended up hitting several other vehicles before running up into a yard and crashing into a house.

A little later, after her husband got home, the mother called their local priest for some spiritual comfort. The priest told her to say 12 Our Fathers and 12 Hail Mary's and she should feel better. Both were absolutely perplexed at this useless instruction from someone they thought would show them a little compassion and understanding. Finally, the good doctor suggested they call the Protestant church down the street from their house. The pastor, having already seen the news, knew of their anguish. He didn't hesitate for a moment, but simply asked the doctor for their address and was at their house in a matter of minutes.

After a lot of discussion and prayer, this kindly minister suggested that he go to the police station with them as moral support. They gladly accepted his offer and went to the local precinct. They were told to go to the central lock-up, which was downtown next to the courthouse. The parents and minister were permitted to see Junior for ten minutes. During that time, it was apparent that Junior was high. He was belligerent to his parents and especially to the pastor. He went on a tirade of curses and accusations toward his parents that were unfounded and unwarranted.

On the way back home, the pastor saw his opportunity to tell them about Jesus and his great love for them, and yes, even for their son. Before the night was over, both the doctor and his wife made a confession of faith in Jesus Christ and were saved, something that had never happened in their former Catholic church. They had never been taught to confess their sins to Jesus and him alone. They were told to confess to the priest. For the first time in their lives, they both expressed a desire to know more about Jesus and true Christianity and not some "hocus pocus" rituals that had no meaning to them. Three days later, Sunday, they joined this Protestant church and made a public profession of faith. Their other three children joined them in converting to Christianity. A few weeks later, they were all baptized.

Now that things had settled down somewhat and they

knew what the charges would be, the good doctor decided it was time to go back down to the jail and talk to his son. He promised to get him the best lawyer in town but knew that he was facing some serious charges: three counts of 2nd-degree murder and five counts of attempted murder for the other people that had become sick and nearly died. He also faced several counts of drug distribution pending and multiple traffic violations. As the father spoke, the boy just sat there. He never said a single word or even thanked his father for agreeing to stick by him and pay for a lawyer.

In an effort to change the subject and try to break the ice with this wayward son, the doctor began telling his son of their experience with the local priest and how uncaring he had been. He then told him about the Protestant minister and the family, making a profession of faith in Jesus and getting baptized. He tried to explain to his son what a feeling of relief and joy it was for him and the rest of the family; that they now had daily devotions and Bible readings in their home. To the best of his ability, he witnessed to his son, hoping that he, too, would accept Jesus as his savior.

Instead, the boy finally rose to his feet and called the jailer to take him back to his cell. Before he parted ways with his father, he turned, and with a look of pure evil in his eyes, said, "I don't want your Jesus, and I don't need him."

When the doctor got home and told his wife what had happened, he described the look in his son's eyes as almost like flames shooting with pure hatred. Neither of them could understand how this once docile boy had turned into a monster.

Finally, in desperation, they called their minister and told him what had happened. He came to their house and began slowly to explain what he thought the problem was and why he was so upset.

He fully believed that a demon or demons had taken over

their son's life. For anyone to have such hatred toward a parent who is sincerely trying to help them is not rational and can be understood in one of two ways. A biblical way tells us that Satan's demons (fallen angels) will do anything in their power to destroy us. He said, in this case, they had taken control of their son's mind and body. The world's way tells us that we are sick and need therapy and pills. The biblical approach of trusting in Jesus worked two thousand years ago, and it still works today. Man's way takes months or years just to get a person into a somewhat palatable state where he is not a danger to himself or others. Some only become more violent with treatments.

The minister said, "On my way over here tonight, I came under what I believe was a demonic attack like I have never witnessed before in my many years in the ministry. Everything around me was out of control. My car would shut off and then start back up, the brakes would lock up when I hadn't even touched the pedal, and my cell phone started a noise that I had never heard before. I was able to understand what the sound was finally. It was a deep gravelly voice, much like those we hear in horror movies that are depicting evil spirits. This thing kept telling me to turn around. It said to go back home and not to go there. I placed my hand on my Bible that was on the seat next to me, and everything went back to normal. "

A few months later, at the trial, the young man was sentenced to life without parole for the three deaths he had caused. He finally admitted that he had cut the cocaine with a white powder he found in the tool shed where his father kept the lawn equipment and various poisons for weeds or insects. He had mixed a deadly poison with his cocaine to increase the volume so that he could improve his profits. The next day before he was transported to the state prison to begin serving his sentence, he asked if his parents and the minister could see him.

This time he had an entirely different demeanor and asked the minister to pray for him and to send him a Bible. He was different than he had been when his father tried to talk to him soon after his arrest. It was as though the demons had done their dirty work by destroying his life and had moved on to destroying someone else.

QUESTIONS

#5. REBELLIOUS CHILD

1. What kind of husband are you? Do you spend exceptionally long hours working? _____ yes _____ no
   a. If you answered yes, what are you going to do about it?

---

   b. If you answered no, you are to be congratulated.

2. How much time do you spend daily or weekly with your children?
   a. Weekdays _____ hours
   b. Weekends _____ hours

3. If you and your wife have a healthy relationship, arguments and disagreements are going to happen and are normal. However, you should never go to bed while still angry. Do you?
   a. the Husband_____ yes _____ no
   b. the Wife_____ yes _____ no

.

4. Are you willing and able to listen to your children's (his/her) side in an argument and admit when you are wrong?

    a. the Husband _____ yes _____ no

    b. the Wife _____ yes _____ no

LETTER 6

INCESTUOUS FATHER

Papa,

Why did you rape my sisters and me? Because of you, I turned to a life of sin. Papa, when I was almost 14 years old, you came into my bedroom late one night and climbed into bed with me. I was scared and asked what you were doing? You told me that you had noticed that I was becoming a shapely young woman and that I needed to take care of your needs. I had no idea what you meant. It was obvious that you had been drinking, and you started ripping off my nightclothes until I was naked and still trying to get away from you. I was crying profusely and begging you to stop, but you were much too powerful for me, and you had your way with me.

The next morning, I told Mama what you had done. She slapped me and called me a liar, told me to get out of her sight, and that she didn't want to hear any more of my lies about my Papa. I was too scared and ashamed to tell anyone else what had happened. I kept the deep dark secret to myself.

To the Reader:

PAPA KEPT COMING INTO my bedroom every time he got drunk and always had his way with me. I hated him, but I had nowhere to go and no one to turn to for help. For over two years, this terror went on before I got up enough courage to run away from home. I had never been more than 50 miles from home until then, but I hitchhiked to a good-sized city. The first night, I slept in a bus station and wandered around the town during the day. I found some unlocked buildings for the first few days. At least they were warm inside at night. I felt safe until one night; I was sleeping in the ladies' room in a rather large building when the janitor came in. He raped me!

A few days later, I wandered into a barroom to get out of the cold. The bartender offered me some food, for which I was very thankful. He must have noticed how hungry I was and felt sorry for me. He offered me a job cleaning the bar each morning and a place to sleep out of the cold as part of the pay. After a few weeks, I found that I was becoming emotionally attached to him because he was kind and gentle with me. One night, he came into my small bedroom, and we had sex. This became a nightly routine after closing time for a little over a year.

Then one night, he suggested that one of his friends would give me fifty dollars if he could sleep with me. That was more money than I had ever seen at one time in my entire life. It became a weekly arrangement. Word soon got around that I was available for a price, and other men started coming into my bedroom.

After I had saved a good bit of money, I moved to a larger town where I encountered my first real house of prostitution. I went to work there and was entertaining from 10-12 men every night. The money was rolling in even though it was a 60/40 split. At least I got 60%.

Time passed quickly. I had saved a fair bit of money, bought a car, and had some nice clothes when I decided that I would go back home for a few days to visit my sisters and Mama. I didn't want to see Papa, but unfortunately, he was still there.

The first night there, I heard a familiar noise coming from my little sister's bedroom. I went to the door, and sure enough, there was Papa doing her. I broke a table lamp over his head and started screaming at him when my older sister and Mama came running in to see what was happening.

Now Mama had to believe all three of us girls that Papa had been raping us since each one of us turned 14. She could no longer deny the truth, having caught him without any clothes on in my sister's bedroom. Mama called the sheriff, and they came and took Papa away.

I stayed around for the trial. Papa went to prison for statuary rape. Mama cried a lot and drank a lot more than usual. She blamed me for Papa's sins and said that he would never have done those things if I hadn't tempted him. I left.

A few days later, I found myself in a new town and a new house. After a few weeks, I had made friends with one of the other girls. She invited me to go to church with her on a Sunday morning. I had nothing better to do, so I went with her to a big Catholic church. Afterward, I had to hang around and wait for her to go to confession, something I hadn't done since I was 12 years old. For the next several weeks, we went every Sunday. I began to think that perhaps I needed my sins forgiven. I had been sinning for a long time now. So, the next Sunday afternoon, I made my way to the confessional.

I started going to confession almost every week. Finally, this priest asked me over to the parsonage. Once there, he offered me a glass of wine, which I thought was okay because, after all, he was a priest. We shared almost two bottles of wine and ended up in his bed, which was okay because he forgave me of my sins, and Lord knows I had plenty. This relationship went on for about two years until he got transferred. I followed him to his next town, but an older priest kept a tight rein on him, so our affair was over. I was heartbroken because I had fallen in love with this priest. It was the first time in my life that I had really cared for another human being. I became despondent.

There was always plenty of alcohol and drugs around, and I began to use both to excess. As I drank more and more, I became more depressed. The alcohol wasn't enough, so I turned to the drugs for more relief. The final straw came on a Saturday afternoon when I went to church for confession. My priest friend would not hear my confession and sent me away instead. Somehow through the tears, I made it back to the house. Once there, I started taking any kind of pill that was available until one of the girls came in with some heroin. I had never taken heroin before, and I had no idea how much to inject.

I must have overdosed because I awoke with this horrible stench of burning flesh. I looked at my hands, they were on fire, but they didn't burn up. All around me, people were screaming and hollering, even some people that I knew. To my surprise, there were Catholic priests there in the same predicament. I looked around further, and Papa was burning with all the rest of the lost souls. It seems that justice was finally served when he was stabbed to death in prison. Here he is, justice at last.

After some time had passed, Papa came to me and told me how sorry he was for the things he had done to my sisters and me.

MAMA,

I forgave him, for what good it did either of us. At least I was aware that I was in this awful place not because of what

Papa had done to me or what the priest had done to me but because of what I had let my circumstances do to me. I had the opportunity to walk away and stay on the straight-and-narrow road that leads to salvation. Instead, I chose the path of least resistance and can blame only myself.

Return to the letter:

Mama, I can only beg of you to get out of that demon-possessed church and find a real Bible-believing church and turn to Jesus. Do not come to this awful place, this hell.

QUESTIONS

#6. INCESTUOUS FATHER

1. As a father of young girls, have you ever had sexual thoughts about your daughters? _____ yes _____ no

If you answered yes to this question, you need serious professional help, now.

2. Mothers, if one of your daughters came to you and told you of improper sexual advances being made toward them by their father, a relative, or anyone, would you take immediate action to protect them and punish the perpetrator? _____ yes _____ no

3. If you answered yes, what action would you take?

a. Do nothing at all and not believe my daughter

_____ yes _____ no

b. Confront the accused person

_____ yes _____ no

c. Call the police and turn them in

_____ yes _____ no

4. Mothers, if this happened in your family, would you continue to stay in a marriage with this person?

_____ yes . _____ no

5. What if it were your teenage son or another relative? Would you take action as suggested in steps b. & c. in question # 3 above?

_____ yes _____ no

LETTER 7

UNINTERESTED PARENTS

Mom/Dad,

Why didn't you teach me about Jesus? Why didn't you tell me about hell? Why? Was it because you didn't know Jesus yourself, or was it because you just didn't care? Was it because you didn't believe the Bible and what it taught? I don't ever remember seeing you read a Bible. I do remember you had to call your mom to get a Bible for me to take to a summer camp. There must not have been one in our home before that. Maybe there was, and I just didn't pay attention. Was it because you were too busy trying to "get ahead" or keep up with the neighbors to pay attention to my spiritual growth? You did everything for my educational growth. Were you too busy with all your hobbies, your trips, and your parties that were just excuses to get drunk? Why was it that you always had time for your friends but never time for my spiritual training? Why Mom? Why Dad? Why were the golf course, boating, or cars and motorcycles more important on Sunday morning than taking me to church to learn about Jesus? Why did you always dump us on Grandma every year after Christmas so you could go to some lake in another state to be with your friends? As we got older, why couldn't you have taken us with you? Why couldn't you have spent New Year's Eve and New Years' day with us so that we could celebrate as a family? I finally realized what was going on when I heard you telling someone on the phone how Dad stayed up almost all night drinking with a friend, and you had to drive back home the next day because Dad was too hungover to drive.

I remember you saying you didn't believe what the preachers were saying; that all they wanted was our money so they could live a high and mighty life, telling others what to do or not do without really having to work themselves. I do remember you scoffing at our neighbors when they invited us to their church on a Sunday morning. You wouldn't let me go. You said: "I would have to get up too early to get you ready, and I usually didn't feel like getting up early on Sunday mornings anyway." However, I must compliment you, Mom and Dad, as you gave me the best of everything while I was growing up. You gave me the latest and greatest toys, the nicest clothes, and the fastest cars. You gave me anything and everything that I wanted except the one thing that I needed most. You saw to it that I always had a pocket full of money and a great education. You gave me everything except the knowledge of Jesus, and that was what I needed more than anything.

To the Reader:

Time seemed to fly by, and Dad was the first to go because of the lifestyle he had lived. He burned himself out. Mom passed away shortly after that from some disease. We didn't have a church service for Dad or Mom, just a memorial service at the funeral home. Most of us went to a bar afterward for a few drinks to remember the good times. Later that day, after the memorial, I thought a little about those two services and thought to myself, we didn't even know a preacher or a church where we could have had a service. But what the heck. I knew Dad wouldn't have felt right lying in a coffin in a church of all places. And I knew that Mom didn't care either way.

Over the next few years, I lived my life almost as recklessly as Dad had lived his. I was drinking a lot more. I look back and remember lying in bed, staring at the ceiling in the dark with an emptiness that I couldn't explain. It was like a vacuum from deep within. The more material things I acquired, the more I wanted. I was never satisfied, and I always felt as though something was missing in my life, but I couldn't understand what it was. I was yearning for something but did not understand what. Perhaps, just perhaps, that small voice calling out to me in the middle of the night was the voice of the Holy Spirit trying to get through to me. Somewhere from the fog and depth of my mind, I vaguely remember hearing a song on TV one Sunday morning, *Softly and tenderly Jesus is calling, calling for you and for me, oh sinner come home, come home*; I was too stubborn to listen. I turned the TV off.

Not long after these thoughts began to permeate my psyche, I had my first heart attack. The doctors said that I was fortunate to have survived and that I needed to drastically change my lifestyle. I took their advice. I switched from drinking whiskey to vodka, less smell on the breath. Then I had my second heart attack.

This time I didn't make it.

~

MOM AND DAD,

I'm in hell, a place that is far worse than anyone can imagine. But I suppose you already know that because I am sure that you are somewhere here as well.

Now that it is too late, I can see things a lot more clearly than ever before. I suppose that is what we often called hindsight. I look back and blame you, Mom and Dad, for me being here in this awful place, and I hate you for not leading me to Jesus when I was young and impressionable. If you had only cared for all your children enough to learn about Jesus and teach us, maybe, just maybe, I wouldn't be here, and neither would you.

I was thinking about how long eternity is. I remember learning in school that dinosaurs were roaming the earth 30,000,000, 40,000,000, possibly 50,000,000 years ago. Eternity goes way back beyond that. It means that being in hellfire and torment for all of eternity will be much longer. It is more than the finite human mind can comprehend.

Mom/Dad, I have learned much since I have been in this awful place. For one thing, Satan can quote the entire Bible, verse by verse, and one of his favorites to quote and make fun of us with is Proverbs 22:6

> *"Train up a child in the way he should go: and when he*
> *is old, he will not depart from it."*

Now I can see as plain as day if you had told us of Jesus and his love, I might not be here today and forever. I can only hope that somehow my younger brother finds Jesus, accepts him as his savior and does not end up here.

But I have slowly learned something else since I have been in this place of torment. I am here because I didn't listen to that still small voice that kept trying to reach me for so many years. I am here because I wouldn't listen to any of my friends when they attempted to tell me about Jesus. I am here because I rejected Christ and His saving grace. I guess what I am trying to say is that I am here in hell because I deserve to be here. It is my own fault, and

Mom/Dad, I forgive you even though it is too late.

QUESTIONS

#7. UNINTERESTED PARENTS

1. What kind of parent are you? Are you a (a) Christian, (b) non-believer, (c) agnostic?

    a. the Father (a) _____ (b) _____ (c) _____

    b. the Mother (a) _____ (b) _____ (c) _____

2. Do you and your spouse attend Church and take your children to Church? _____ yes _____ no

3. If you answered "no" to the above question, why not?

    _____ yes _____ no

4. Are your (friends, toys, boats, motorcycles, sports, etc.) * partying more important than your children's eternal soul and salvation? _____ yes _____ no

5. Would you, as a parent, tell your children to "go to hell?" Of course, not, but in a way, by neglecting their spiritual growth and knowledge, that is just what you are doing. When a child grows up without a Christian foundation at home, he/she is

unlikely to find Jesus and His saving grace on their own. What changes do you need to make in your and their lives?

_____

_____

_____

*All of these can be idols in your life.

LETTER 8

MOM, YOU TAUGHT ME THE WILD SIDE
OF LIFE

Mom,

You taught me about having a good time. Why didn't you teach me about Jesus? Mom, I know you thought you were doing the best you could for me when I was young. After all, Dad had walked out on us, and I only saw him a few times while growing up. I know and understand that you were a young, beautiful woman who was extremely lonely, with a young daughter to look after. Mom, the one thing I didn't understand until I was a teenager was why men that kept coming and going at all hours of the night.

I can remember several of my friends asking me to go to church on Sunday mornings or to Vacation Bible School in the summer. You always said no that I didn't need any of that religion stuff. So, I never really had the opportunity to learn about Jesus and His saving grace until it was too late.

You see, Mom, I followed in your footsteps and started having sex with the neighborhood boys when I was about 13, or maybe it was 14. That same year one of the boys introduced me to marijuana. I could smoke a joint and no longer felt guilty about the sex. After a while having sex with several boys at the same time wasn't a big deal. I no longer cared. When I had VD, the free clinic always took care of it. Planned Parenthood provided a solution for my pregnancy when I was 16. You never knew about that.

Then one day, an older man offered me money for sex. I thought, why not I have been giving it away, I should be more like Mom. You see, I had finally figured out why all of the strange men kept coming at all hours of the night and why I couldn't come out of my room, and why there was always a lot of cash on your bedside table the next morning. I could have my pleasure and make a lot of money at the same time, and I was just like you. This went on for several years, the sex and the drugs.

You see, I had graduated from marijuana to cocaine and then to shooting up heroin. I didn't realize how my appearance had changed. I could no longer get the young, affluent johns, but only the down and out bums. I no longer kept or even tried to keep up my appearance. My only thought was getting enough money for my next fix.

Then one night, I overdosed. Luckily the guy I was with called 911 before he left out the back door of the flophouse. When I came to, I was in a hospital hooked up to tubes and machines. Finally, a doctor came in and sat down beside my bed. He said I have something serious to tell you. I will try to be as gentle as I can, but you have full-blown Aids. Yours is a very virulent form that we really can't treat. You probably have only a few weeks to live. We will do everything we can to make you as comfortable as possible. Now, is there anyone you would like for us to contact?

I was in a daze and couldn't think or even remember your address or phone number. I had gone my own way maybe ten years earlier and had completely lost track of you. I was not even in the same town or state as you. I was all alone.

Mom, when you are dying, time seems to pass as quickly as the clouds or rushing water in a fast-flowing stream.

I passed away late at night. Here I was suddenly in this place with fire and an unknown stench all about me. I saw and heard screaming people, people consumed by fire, but they didn't burn up, they just kept burning and burning. I was experiencing the same thing and finally began to realize where I was and why. There was the devil himself laughing at us and cursing Jesus and everything that is and was Holy. Perhaps this was the first time that I really heard about Jesus and understood why I should have known him while I was alive and had the opportunity to know him. I can't blame you entirely for my being in this awful, awful place.

Mom, I know you had a rough time after Dad left us, but why didn't you turn to a church for help? There were many compassionate people there that could have helped us get over our loss instead of living a life of sin. Why didn't you learn about Jesus and tell me about him? Why, Mom, why? If you had, if I had heard about him, I might not be in this awful place for all of eternity.

In looking back over my life after I was a grown woman, I had many opportunities to turn my life over to the Lord. But in my stubbornness, I rejected what the counselors said when I was arrested and spent some time in jail. The counselors told me about Jesus, and a preacher held services every Sunday that we were required to attend. I have no excuse, no one to blame but myself for rejecting Christ.

Eternity, Mom! Eternity is more than the human mind can comprehend. This fire, the sores, the smells, and the screams are more than any of us can bear, but we have no choice. This torment goes on day after day, night after night because there is no such thing as sleep here.

I know that my letter to you from this hellish place can never reach you, but I can hope that you will turn to Jesus before it is too late for you. I can only hope, and even though it is too late for me, maybe I can pray for you even from here.

QUESTIONS

#8. MOM, YOU TAUGHT ME THE WILD SIDE OF LIFE

1. If your marriage broke up today, would you follow this mother's example? _____ yes_____ no

2. What would you do differently?
   a. Get a job to support myself. _____ yes_____ no
   b. Reach out to family or friends for advice and help?
   _____ yes_____ no

3. Turn to or find a Bible-believing church to attend?
   _____ yes_____ no

4. If children are involved, would that make a difference in how you would respond? _____ yes_____ no

5. Have you accepted Jesus Christ as your savior?
   _____ yes_____ no

6. Do you belong to a church? _____ yes_____ no

7. Do you think that if you and your husband had been Christians and attending church regularly, your marriage would have broken up? _____ yes_____ no

LETTER 9

DEAR EX-HUSBAND

Dear ex-husband,

Because of you, I destroyed myself, my mom, and your daughter. Aren't you proud? I learned one thing yesterday, no, I learned two things: 1- a human being can't flap her arms and fly from a twentieth story balcony and not go straight down, and 2- there is a place called hell, and I am here in it. I vaguely remember something from a Sunday school lesson when I was a little girl about a rich man pleading with God for a beggar to place a drop of water on his tongue. I would give anything if I could only have a small drop of water, just once. It is unbelievable here, the flames, the smells, the screams, and the crying. We all want to die again and sink into nothingness like the vacuum of space, anything but this unimaginable place. There is continual torment—there is no night and day in this place with the flames being brighter than looking up at the noonday sun.

I look back at you, dear husband, and remember how you cursed and slapped me around before throwing me out of the house because I had scorched your favorite bowling shirt. You pushed me out the door and told me never to come back. You had done this many times before when you had been drinking, but somehow this time, I knew you meant it. I was deeply, emotionally hurt.

TO THE READER:

As I wandered aimlessly down the street, I passed a small church on the corner. I paused for a few minutes to hear singing gently wafting through the open windows. I almost went in, but something kept telling me, "you don't belong with these people; you just need a drink to settle your nerves."

So, I wandered on down the street for a few blocks until I ran across a cocktail lounge. Cocktail lounge! Now that sounded a lot better than a bar. I went in. It was ladies' night, so I could drink for free unless someone was buying a drink for me, a man, of course. After a few drinks, I was feeling no pain from my earlier troubles when a very polite nice-looking man came over and sat down beside me. We talked and drank for another hour or so when he finally asked me if I lived around here? I told him what had happened earlier in the evening and mentioned that I had no place to go or stay. He invited me to his place for the night.

I thought, why not? The bum I am married to doesn't want me, and this guy does, so I went with him.

For the first time in my life, I broke my marriage vows that night, enjoying myself for the first time in years. I ended up staying with this man for several weeks while trying to sort out what I was going to do long-term. I went back to the house during the day while my dear husband was at work, got my clothes, and took one of the cars. I wondered what I would live on when I hit upon an idea—why not sell myself for money. I enjoyed sex for the first time in over 15 years, and I was still in pretty good shape and not too bad looking.

I started making the rounds of several bars and letting myself get "picked up." The money was good, especially if I worked all night and didn't spend too much time with any one man. Soon I had enough money put aside to rent my own apartment and start building a life for myself and all without having to work a nine to five tedious office job.

The years passed, and I was still having a good time and making a lot of money. I had bought a nice condo on the right side of the tracks. That was my sanctuary; no johns allowed. I maintained a working apartment where I conducted business along with occasionally one or two other girls. None of these were permanent, just passing through for a day or two. I did have to keep changing work apartments frequently because neighbors would start to get nosy and ask questions about all the different men that kept coming and going at all hours.

About this time, my Mom came up to visit from Florida. I brought her to the condo at first, but in my degenerated mind, I decided to take her to my work apartment. I wanted more than anything to drag her down to my level after all the things she said to me after my marriage broke up. According to her, it was entirely my fault. We could talk and visit in between my customers.

After the third "boyfriend" came and went, dear old Mom had figured out what was taking place. She was appalled. I laughed it off and asked her how long it had been since she was with a man? Dad had passed away about 15 years ago, and Mom still lived in her big old house all alone. She finally admitted that she had been with a couple of guys a time or two, but nothing regular. I suggested she join in with me.

She was mortified at first. After a day or two of thinking about it, she announced that she wanted to give it a try. Mom was in her early 50's, almost 5'11" and maybe 155 pounds, and well endowed. I knew that some of my regular customers would want her, and they did. She made herself available to three the first night. I had now totally corrupted myself and my own mother, leaving only one more to be brought down.

When my dear husband divorced me several years ago, I made sure that all our old friends and his relatives knew what profession I had gone into and that it was his fault. I wanted to blame anyone and everyone but myself and wanted to embarrass him as much as possible. I had one more goal, and that was to turn his daughter into a prostitute when she turned 16, which was the legal age of consent in our state.

The judge in our divorce settlement had given me 30 days of custody each year, and her 16th birthday was coming up. It would be the perfect time to get even. I had one customer that looked like he stepped off the pages of GQ magazine. He was perfect for my ex-husband's daughter and only 25 years old.

I set her up with him and gave her some wine. When I poured her second glass, I slipped in a little pill. After a few minutes, they headed to the bedroom. She spent the rest of the night with him and the next night as well. I managed to sneak into the room and take a few Polaroid photos for her dear daddy.

A few months after her introduction to life's wicked pleasures, she and another girl moved into their own apartment and set up shop. Her dear daddy was about to lose his mind over his daughter's downfall. He expressed this along with a tirade of curses directed at me. Her apartment didn't last very long as she got busted after a few weeks. The neighbors got tired of the wild parties, loud music, and drugs that were always present.

My revenge on my dear ex-husband was now complete, and I could relax and revel. However, my gloating soon came to an end. It was the early 1970s, and drugs were flowing freely, especially LSD. I was at a party in a penthouse on the 20th floor of a downtown building. We were all drinking heavily and smoking a few joints when someone slipped some LSD into one of my drinks.

I was standing close to the sliding glass doors leading onto the balcony when I started to see all these colorful clouds floating by. I had to get closer, so I went onto the balcony. Then I decided that I wanted to soar with the birds and the clouds. That is when I learned that a human being cannot fly by jumping off a tall building and frantically flapping their arms. Amazingly you go straight down and keep on going right into the bottomless pit called hell.

Dear ex-husband,

From this bottomless pit, I blame you for all that has happened to me, Mom, and your daughter. I was a good, loyal, and faithful wife to you for the entire time we lived together. You got mad over a $10.00 bowling shirt and threw me out of the house and, in a sense, out of everything I had ever believed. Everything I had hoped for or dreamed about all my life vanished in a moment of your anger.

Because of you, I turned into the evilest and vile thing that a woman can become. Even worse, in my anger, I corrupted my own mother and your beautiful daughter. Even today, with all of the rage I had built up toward you, I can only hope and pray that you will repent of your sins. Do not come to this awful place.

Hopefully, you can persuade your daughter to accept Christ and not end up here.

Finally, after some time in this torment, I have come to

realize that I am here because of my own sins. It is not something you did to me or something Mom did to me but what I did to myself. If only I had turned and gone into that little church the night so long ago when you threw me out of the house. I might, no, I probably wouldn't be in this horrid place. I now know that it is too late to realize that those people in that little church on a Wednesday night were, in a sense calling out to me to "come to the cross," but I was too angry at you to listen.

Oh, that I had just listened to their call.

QUESTIONS

#9. DEAR EX-HUSBAND

1. You ordered me out of the house because I scorched your favorite bowling shirt, was that the real reason?

_____ yes_____ no

2. What was the real reason? Did you find someone else?

_____ yes_____ no

3. I turned to prostitution because you had never allowed me to work, and I didn't have any other way to earn money?

_____ yes_____ no

4. I had always been a good and faithful wife; were you always faithful to me?

_____ yes_____ no

5. I have let all our former friends know what has become of me; are you the least bit embarrassed?

_____ yes_____ no

6. I hated my own mother because she took your side and abandoned me; I corrupted her, are you happy with that?

_____ yes_____ no

7. What about our daughter at 16 becoming a hooker? Aren't you proud of her?

_____ yes_____ no

8. Are you or do you know someone in this same type situation?

_____ yes_____ no

JACK THE PHILANDERER

Jack was a handsome young man in his late twenties and a very successful used car salesman in a large southern city. Jack had everything going his way, a substantial income with plenty of time off to pursue his other interests. He was a "sharp" dresser and liked to keep up with the latest fashions. He usually looked as though he had just stepped off the pages of GQ magazine. As a salesman, Jack excelled in his profession. People said he could probably sell ice to an Eskimo. Jack's success went on for several years, and it seemed that he was happy with his lot in life.

On the other side of the proverbial coin, Jack had a beautiful wife and a daughter who had just become a teenager. They lived in an exclusive housing complex that provided almost every amenity that a young family could want: two swimming pools, several putting greens for the golfers, indoor/outdoor tennis courts, and a clubhouse with most of the latest indoor games for the kids to enjoy. It was an ideal place for Jack and his wife to raise their daughter. They did not have to worry about her safety in this gated community. If a stranger were to look at Jack and his little family, they might see an idyllic life, but there was something beneath the surface that wasn't right.

Jack had a mistress on the side, a beautiful young divorcee with a teenage daughter. Jack would leave work around 6:00 pm every day and go to his girlfriend's house for dinner. She usually cooked, or they might go out to a high-end restaurant in town.

Jack was seen with this woman and her daughter so often that most people thought she was his wife. Jack spent all his spare time with his girlfriend and even took vacations with her and her daughter several times a year. They went to places like New Orleans or Disney World for a week at a time. The sad part was that his own daughter had begged him many times to take her to Disney World, but Jack always had an excuse.

Another thing about Jack; he never took his wife or daughter out to eat, or if he did, it was usually to a drive-in with curbside service. The truth is that as a husband and father, Jack was a louse and didn't deserve the trusting wife he had.

Jack's girlfriend knew all about Jack's wife and daughter and the way he treated them. She thought, "She must be the stupidest woman alive."

This farce went on for several years, with Jack getting away with deceiving his wife and living a double life. Eventually, Jack's daughter and the girlfriend's daughter both entered the 9th grade and had a gym class together. There was still no problem because neither girl knew the other one existed until one day, the girlfriend's daughter dropped her wallet.

Jack's daughter picked it up to hand it back when she suddenly saw a picture of Jack, the girlfriend, and her daughter standing in front of Cinderella's castle at Disney World. Even though she was shocked beyond belief, she had the forethought to play dumb and ask who the people were in the photo. The girlfriend's daughter innocently replied that it was her, of course, her Mom and her Mom's boyfriend. The next question was, when were you at Disney World?

The unsuspecting girl told her that they had spent a week "down there" last summer and that they were going back around Thanksgiving for another week.

Jack's daughter was beginning to understand a lot more than she wanted to know, but she pressed on and asked her if they had taken any more-great vacations like that one? The girlfriend's daughter began to tell all in a bragging sort of way, the trips to New Orleans, Nashville, and several trips to Panama City Beach.

Jack's daughter couldn't wait to get home and tell her mom what she had learned. Then they sat down at the table and began going through a calendar marking the dates that Jack had gone deep-sea fishing or deer hunting or to an automobile dealer's convention. That was his favorite excuse. There seemed to be a lot of conventions that he just had to attend. By the time they had finished putting everything together, they had figured that Jack and this woman had taken over a dozen vacations in the last two years, but his own daughter and wife had not been on a single vacation with him.

Jack's wife had some serious decisions to make, so she called her sister to come and get her daughter and take her for a few days, possibly longer. Next, she went to the bank and cleaned out the checking and savings accounts, and got a check made out to her daughter.

After leaving there, she went home and waited for the philanderer to come back. Jack finally came in about 11:30, as usual. Unlike most nights, she asked him where he had been. As usual, Jack had a terrific tale about why he was so late. This time, the problem was that his sweet little wife didn't accept his word and just go to bed for some unknown reason. Instead, she called him a liar. How could this be happening after all this time? Jack was astounded she called him a liar. He simply didn't understand how this could be. Hadn't he always covered his tracks? Jack tried to play dumb, but the jig was up. He had been caught. Not only had Jack's wife found out who this other woman was, but she had also taken pictures of Jack going into her house and sitting out back on the patio with her on his lap. Also, she had waited until Jack had left her at 9:15 and confronted her.

She admitted the entire sordid affair. Jack's "goose was cooked." Unknown to him, he would soon be joining his beloved girlfriend in hell. In a fit of anger, Jack got up and started threateningly across the room when his darling wife pulled a pistol out of a paper bag and fired five shots right into Jack's chest. There was a look of complete shock and amazement on his face as he fell to the floor, dead. His wife stood over him and told his corpse that now he could be together forever with his darling girlfriend. She then calmly picked up the phone and called the police to report two murders, one Jack's mistress and the other "her no-good husband."

A strange thing happened. Even in death, Jack could not escape the wrath of this good and terribly wronged woman, his wife. He seemed to be floating near the ceiling, looking down as the apartment flooded with police and EMS crews that tried to revive him to no avail. The coroner arrived, pronounced him dead, and had his body picked up by a funeral home.

Jack's wife was finally handcuffed and taken to jail. The next day she was charged and arraigned on two counts of 1st-degree murder and held without bail. Several months passed, and finally, her trial was scheduled, a jury was picked, and the prosecutor made his case, which seemed as though it would be a slam dunk guilty verdict. All the while, old Jack was floating above the courtroom, watching and listening, and sometimes trying to interject his thoughts and words into the proceedings, but no one heard him. It was very frustrating.

Finally, the defense had their opportunity to present their case before the jury. Jack's wife's attorney laid out a case of Jack's philandering for most of their married life and how he had neglected both his wife and daughter but spent lavishly on the girlfriend and her daughter.

Jack's daughter was called to the stand, and she told how she accidentally learned of her dad's indiscretions with "the other woman" and her daughter. She told of begging him to take her to Disney World, but he had an excuse year after year. She told of going out to dinner occasionally with her dad and always to a drive-in restaurant with carhops and having to eat in the car. When she was asked by the prosecutor if she was sorry, her mother had killed her dad; her answer was an immediate, "NO! I am glad that he is dead and out of our lives. The only thing that I regret is that my mom will probably go to prison." The two attorneys did their summations, and the judge sent the jury out to deliberate. Now, Jack was still floating above the courtroom and was feeling jubilant at the thought of his wife finally getting her just due and spending the rest of her life in prison.

After about 90 minutes had passed, the jury sent word to the judge that they had reached a unanimous verdict. Everyone came back into the courtroom to await the sentencing. Jack was ecstatic at the thought of seeing his wife in prison garb. The judge read the verdict and asked the jury if this was their final verdict and if all concurred? They all answered in the affirmative, yes. The judge then told the foreman to read their verdict, which he did. "We, the jury, find this defendant not guilty due to extreme cruelty on the part of her husband that drove her to take such drastic measures." The judge thanked the jury for their service and told Jack's wife that she was free to go home to her daughter.

Jack could not believe what he was seeing and hearing, but that was the least of his troubles. He was immediately thrown into the lake of fire in torment and anguish over what he had done to his wife and daughter for all those years. To him, this "hell" was unfathomable, and then his old girlfriend found him and began cursing him for leading her astray many years ago.

As was usual, when someone first realizes where he or she is, they want to blame everyone they have ever known for their predicament that is everyone but themselves. Jack wanted to blame his wife, and in his perverted mind, Jack reasoned that he had given her the best of everything that money could buy. A new car of her choice every year, the most expensive clothes and anything else she could want. He had his girlfriend right next to him in torment to blame, and he had his former wife that was finally beginning to enjoy life without him, to blame. Jack blamed his daughter for telling her mother about the picture she saw of Jack, the girlfriend, and her daughter standing in front of Cinderella's castle in Disney World. Finally, in despair, he thought to himself, *maybe if I had just taken them to Disney World just once, I wouldn't be in this dreadful place today. I wish that I had.*

Later as some time had passed, Jack began to think back about the many times he had lied to his wife and the many times he had cheated with other women. He finally began to see himself for what he was while alive. He finally admitted to himself that he had become a no-good, lying, abusive philanderer who was not worthy of having the faithful wife he had. He was beginning to think, *oh, if I only had another chance, everything would be different. I would be a model husband and father.* He realized that his wish could never be and that it was his fault that he was in this place of eternal torment.

Jack's final thought before we leave him to suffer alone was that he wanted to somehow communicate to his daughter and her mother to tell them both how sorry he was for the way he had treated them. He hoped against hope that they would realize how much his thinking had changed since he arrived in this place; he was guilty and now extremely remorseful. Jack would hold on to that single thought for the rest of eternity.

QUESTIONS

#10. JACK THE PHILANDERER

1. If you are married, are you faithful to your spouse?

_____ yes_____ no

2. To the best of your knowledge, is your spouse faithful to you?

_____ yes_____ no

3. Are you staying married because children are involved?

_____ yes_____ no

4. Are you or your spouse a Christian?

_____ yes_____ no
_____wife_____husband

5. What would be the reaction of the aggrieved party if he/she learned of the affair? (Check the one that applies)

A. Separation _____

B. Divorce _____

c. Shot _____

D. Nothing _____

6. Are you planning on keeping "status-quo"?

_____ yes_____ no

7. Do you have a friend in a similar situation to Jack's situation?

_____ yes_____ no

8. If you answered yes, what are you going to do to help rectify a situation that should not be happening?

    a. Try talking to my friend. _____ yes _____ no

    b. Tell his spouse about the affair? _____ yes_____ no

    c. Do/say nothing? _____ yes_____ no

LETTER 11

CHARLES GOES TO PRISON

There was a boy that I knew while going to elementary and Jr. High school. He lived across the street from my cousin, and we all played together after school and during the summer. Charles seemed to be a good kid, polite and doing well in school. He and I went to a large church a few blocks from his house and attended almost every Sunday. Then, when we all started the 9th grade, Charles stopped coming to Sunday school and church. As was the custom in those simpler times, our class had a group that visited those who missed more than five Sundays in a row. We visited Charles, and his mother was astounded that he had not been going to Sunday school and church. He would get up on Sunday morning, as usual, get dressed and leave the house, telling his mother that he was going to Sunday school. Instead, Charles was stopping at a neighborhood park about halfway to the church. He would stay there and hang out with some unsavory characters that were several years older than him. It became evident to everyone that these thugs were up to no good, and they were dragging Charles right along with them into a life of petty crime. Several years passed, and we didn't see Charles much anymore. He was too busy with "his gang," as he called them. Charles did manage to graduate from high school with most of us. That was the last we saw of him until one night he showed up on television in handcuffs, being led to a police car. He was the leader of a gang of burglars known locally as the "Hole in the Roof Gang." In those years, the early 1960s, many stores in the strip malls did not have alarm systems except maybe on the doors. Charles and his "boys" would climb up on the roof, cut a hole in it, and climb down a rope ladder to gain entrance.

In most cases, they could spend a lot of time inside because no alarm sounded. These guys went a step further. They had a lookout, with a surplus walkie-talkie, parked across the parking lot to watch for the police or mall security. They were so successful with these burglaries that they had the local police completely stumped. The gang would take their time, gather the "loot" by the back door, then call for their lookout driver to come and pick them up with everything they had stolen. The gang especially went after sporting goods stores for the guns and the office supply/machine stores. The electric typewriters had just debuted in the late 1950s and were a hot seller on the streets. This gang of thieves seemed almost invincible until one night they got careless. They had broken into a large sporting goods store and had several crates of pistols ready to take out the back door. The thing they had overlooked was that this strip mall was "L" shaped. Their lookout couldn't see one end of the alley where the police had blocked the exit. The gang called for their getaway car to come to the back door. They pushed it open, and of course, the alarm sounded. As usual, they thought they would load up the loot and be long gone before the cops got there. They were wrong this time. Everyone hopped into the two cars and sped down the alley. Suddenly, they were confronted with bright lights and flashing blue lights in front of them and behind them at the same time. They were caught. With a building on one side, a high fence with barbed wire on the other, and the police now pointing multiple shotguns at them, they surrendered.

Now a sensational trial took place featuring a childhood friend as a defendant. The whole story came out about their many burglaries and exploits. Besides the gang of thieves, several other people were indicted for fencing the stolen merchandise. A lot of the guns and most of the IBM electric typewriters were recovered. When the court completed their stolen merchandise audit, these guys had taken goods valued at over a million dollars. About $300,000 worth of merchandise was recovered.

Now, because Charles and his friends were all over 18 years of age, they were tried in Superior Court and received sentences ranging from 15 to 35 years each. Charles was sentenced to 25 years plus one week as the gang leader. Why was the one week added, you might ask? In other words, he would have to serve the full 25 years first— before he could serve the one week.

Charles was interviewed by many different people on the prison staff before he was assigned his work detail. Among those was the prison Chaplain. Charles expressed his absolute disdain for anything to do with the church, God, or the Bible. In his sick mind, he blamed God for him being in this place. The chaplain told him that he could go back to his cell and that a trustee would escort him. Then the chaplain tried to hand Charles a Bible, which he refused. After a short tirade of cursing the chaplain for offering him a Bible and cursing the Bible itself, the chaplain had had enough of this little punk. The good Reverend stood up behind his desk and glared at Charles for what seemed like an eternity before finally speaking. He said, "Young man, you did things your way on the outside, and your best thinking got you here where you will spend the next twenty-five years of your life if you can stay alive that long. With your attitude, I doubt that you will make it. Now let's get something straight. You will address all prison personnel as sir, yes sir or no, sir no. If you must walk in front of a guard or another of the uniformed personnel, you will say excuse me, sir, and then after passing, you will say thank you, sir, or ma'am. Also, you will take this Bible back to your cell right now, or you will spend one week in solitary on bread and water. You have a choice." Charles reluctantly picked up the Bible and returned to his cell.

The inmate cells in his wing of the prison held 2 two men per cell, but for the first several weeks, Charles was in the cell by himself. One night after supper Charles needed to use the toilet, which he did. After he had completed his mission, he noticed that there was no toilet paper on the spool. The rule was that you had to turn in the empty cardboard spool to get a new roll of paper. By now, it was after hours, so he could not get another roll before tomorrow morning. What was he to do? Charles looked around and spotted the Bible lying on the spare bunk. In his deranged way of thinking, this was just so much paper going to waste. He tore a few pages out and used them to clean himself. This practice lasted for about two weeks because he was too lazy to take the empty spool to the supply room and get another roll of toilet paper.

Late one evening, Charles was sitting on the toilet just finishing up when another inmate walked by and saw him tearing pages out of the Bible to use for toilet paper. Now you must remember that there is no right to privacy in prison. The toilet was stainless steel, bolted to the wall. This man became enraged, seeing the desecration of the Holy Bible. One thing Charles learned very quickly was that there are many devout Christians in prison. Many men and women find salvation after having their freedom taken away for their actions and sins on the outside. There were some threats made, which Charles just laughed off.

Charles's story all happened in the state of Mississippi, at a huge prison in the delta called Parchman State Penitentiary for Men. Besides being a place of internment, it is a substantial cotton producing plantation. Many of the fields had rows of cotton a mile long, with as many as 250 rows in each field. The inmates were usually placed one man to a row, and it was possible to fill a sack with 100 pounds of cotton before the inmate reached the end of the row.

Up until the late 1970s, all cotton was picked by inmates the old fashioned way, using a long canvas sack with a strap that went over one shoulder, which the inmate pulled beside/behind himself while straddling the cotton plants. Each bag held about 100-125 pounds of cotton. The prison had rules for picking cotton. The number one rule was that each inmate was required to pick a minimum of 100 pounds each day. Charles noticed that some inmates who had grown up on cotton plantations would have their 100 pounds by noon. For this effort, they received $1. If they chose, they could be through for the day and return to the dormitory. However, they could stay and pick another 100 pounds for $2 more. These guys were usually through by 3-4 pm every day. Charles found out the hard way that if he didn't make his quota by 5 pm, the regular time to quit work for the day, he had to stay until the quota was met, meaning he missed supper. Each day at 11:30 am, the chow wagon came to the fields and brought lunch to the inmates. They were allowed 30 minutes for lunch, and there were pavilions scattered about the fields with tables and benches for their use. After working in the fields for about two weeks, Charles began making his quota by 4-4:30 every day, this made life a little easier.

Finally, they had worked their first field out and moved to the next one. There was already a crew working there, and to Charles' astonishment, there was the Christian inmate that had threatened him about desecrating the Bible. As they passed one another, the inmate grinned at him and said, "Thus, saith the Lord (and me), vengeance is mine." Nothing out of the ordinary happened for the first few days besides the hot sun bearing down and the back-breaking work. Finally, on the 3rd day, Charles was about a third of the way down his row. Most of the others were about halfway or farther down their respective rows. The guards on horseback had ridden to the end of the rows where some large trees provided shade. Suddenly Charles found himself surrounded by fellow inmates, led by the angry inmate who had witnessed his ripping the pages from the Bible. Charles tried to run away, but there were too many. They kept knocking him down until suddenly, he felt extreme pain in his neck as one of the men behind him slit his throat from ear to ear. They left him between two rows putting the cotton he had already picked in one of the other inmates' sacks. It took several hours for all the inmates to reach the end of the rows, at which time the guards realized that one was missing. Finally, after much grumbling, they started to search for Charles until they finally found his dead body.

Charles didn't understand what was happening to him. He fell down a long black tunnel and bounced from one side to the other with arms and legs flailing. There was an eerie silence except for the lone sound of a rushing wind that grew louder the farther he fell. Finally, after what seemed like a long time, he landed on his feet in what seemed like a furnace. Suddenly Charles awoke from what he thought had been a dream and realized that, yes, there really is a place called Hell, and he was now in it. He began screaming and crying uncontrollably but to no avail. As his eyes cleared a little, he could see many other people in the same predicament, all crying or screaming in torment. He realized that there were men and women and many teenagers of both sexes, all experiencing the same fate.

A funny thought began to take hold of Charles' memory; he began to recall verbatim the many Sunday school lessons and scripture readings he had heard as a young boy. He remembered all of them as if he was hearing them now for the first time. Especially he remembered John 3:16-18,

> "For God so loved the world that he gave his only
> begotten Son, that whosoever believeth in Him
> should not perish, but have everlasting life. For
> God sent not his Son into the world to condemn the
> world; but that the world through Him might be
> saved. He that believeth on him is not condemned;
> but he that believeth not is condemned already
> because he hath not believed in the name of the only
> begotten Son of God."

Charles could not get these verses out of his mind but kept reciting them repeatedly for what seemed like days and days. As he looked around at the other lost souls, just like him, they were all reciting Bible verses in between spells of uncontrollable crying or screaming. Then Charles thought about his loved ones that were still alive. He was finally thinking about someone other than himself and wanted to reach out to his mother and father. He knew that his mother was saved, but his father had bragged about being a heathen. He didn't need to worry about his younger sister because she was a paragon of virtue and a devout Christian.

Charles remembered that in the Parable of Lazarus and the Rich Man, Jesus said,

"And besides all this, between you and us is a great
gulf fixed: so that they that would pass from hence
to you cannot; neither can they pass to us, that
would come from thence." (Luke 16:26).

Charles was exasperated about how he could get a message back to his wayward father, friends, and relatives. Finally, he realized that in Luke 16:28b-31, Jesus said,

"...that he may testify unto them, lest they also come
unto this place of torment. Abraham saith unto
him, they have Moses and the prophets; let them
hear them, and he said, Nay, Father Abraham: but
if one went unto them from the dead, they would
repent. And he said unto him, if they hear not
Moses and the prophets, neither will they be
persuaded, though one rose from the dead."

With these verses now firmly etched into his memory, Charles finally began to realize that there was nothing he could do to reach out to those still alive. Yet Charles wanted to try to reach out to his mother and father. He looked all around and found several writing stations with paper, envelopes, and pens. Next to each writing station was an old-fashioned phone booth. What irony. Charles opened the door and stepped inside, ready to make a call when he realized that the plastic phone was melted and hanging in threads. With nothing else to do, Charles sat down and wrote a long letter apologizing to his family and friends for the embarrassment he had caused them. However, as soon as he folded his letter and put it into the envelope, it went up in flames. There was nothing to do but try writing another and another, each time with the same result. Charles finally realized that this was another cruel hoax that Satan was playing on all these suffering people. Charles began to grieve heavily over the things he had done and the anguish he had caused those who loved him. It was almost more than he could bear, but now he had no choices. He finally realized that he and he alone had caused all of his problems. His descent into Hell was his fault, and he alone must pay the eternal price for rejecting Jesus and His mercy while he was alive and had the opportunity.

QUESTIONS

11. CHARLES GOES TO PRISON

1. Are you, or do you know someone who is like Charles?

_____ yes_____ no

2. If you answered yes, what do you intend to do about it before it is too late?

    a. Have a long talk with my friend?_____ yes_____ no

    b. Talk to his parents/spouse?_____ yes_____ no

    c. Turn him in to the police?_____ yes_____ no

    d. Do nothing?_____ yes_____ no

3. If the person is not a Christian, will you try to talk to him and win him to Christ? _____ yes_____ no

4. If he refuses to listen, what next?

    a. Pray for him continually?_____ yes_____ no

    b. Ask some of his friends to pray? _____ yes_____ no

    c. Give up on him? _____ yes_____ no

LETTER 12

A MUSLIN SON SPEAKS OUT FROM HELL

Father, as a young child, you taught me to hate all Jews. Why didn't you teach me the truth about them? I found out later in life that you had led me astray in that regard.

Father,

I remember how you and Mother scrimped and saved to send my brother and me to live in the US with an uncle and go to school. After a short time in America, I got a call from you late one night telling me that my mother had passed away. You asked if I could afford to come home to the old country for a few weeks, that you needed me at this stressful time. My wife insisted that I go, but she could not get time off from her job, so I went home alone.

When I got back, my elder cousin, Mohammed, began bragging about killing the Jewish doctor that had delivered his baby and saved his wife's life. He thought it was a badge of honor because the doctor had seen his wife's private parts. It was sort of funny until the Jewish Army came and tore down Mohammed's house and hauled him off to prison for murder. The Palestine Liberation Organization (PLO) gave

Mohammed's wife money to live on for a long time because he was considered a martyr for killing a Jew. It was at this time that I learned how bad things really were in our village. It was then that I decided to stay and fight for the cause with my brothers and cousins.

As boys, we would set tires on fire and roll them down the hills toward the Jewish army posts. When that got old, we would throw stones at the Jewish soldiers, police officers, or school children.

Looking back, father, I remember as a child sitting at your knee listening to you and my uncles talk about their desire to kill the Jews that lived across the valley from us. You and some of my uncles would often slip out of the house, crossing the valley to burn houses and hurt people who had never done anything to us.

Then the violence escalated against the Jews. The Jews would build fences and walls, and our people would dig tunnels. They could break through an old building or just tunnel up through the ground and throw a few grenades and disappear back into the tunnels. I don't know how many of those Jews were killed. They wounded a lot, many of them seriously, with bombs and knives, or by shooting when they had guns and ammunition. While in my mid 20's I joined a rocket brigade. We would move our crude rocket launcher into school-yards and fire away; we knew the Israelis would not shoot back at us for fear of hitting children. Hospitals and Mosques were also good launching sites.

Finally, the Israelis got tired of our constant barrages and invaded our country, wiping out a buffer zone between us. They tore down every house and building for about a quarter of a mile. We still had our tunnels, just a lot longer now. We thought that we were getting away with something until one night, after sneaking under their fence and setting off several explosives, the Israelis collapsed our tunnel behind us, and we were trapped. We had no choice but to surrender. The Jewish judge gave us each ten years in the prison for the "devastation" we had caused. There were six of us in a tiny cell sleeping on the floor and getting fed twice a day. Life was miserable.

After serving a little over three years, they traded us for a couple of captured Israeli soldiers. We were free at last and determined to make those Jews pay; after all, wasn't Allah in charge and didn't, he demand revenge.

Within a few weeks, we had a plan to exact revenge by blowing up a school bus loaded with Jewish kids and then fight our way back home. There was one problem. The Israelis had intercepted some of our communications and were waiting for us. In the pitched gun battle, I was shot through the head and died almost immediately.

Wow, now I am a real martyr in the service of Allah, but dead just the same. But wait, something is very wrong; where are my 72 virgins, where are the date palms and the streams of cool water? This was all promised if I was killed while serving Allah. Why is everything here so hot? Why all the flames, and with all this fire, why am I not being consumed? I hear screaming and grown men crying like babies, what is happening to me? I am supposed to be in paradise; at least that is what the imam's told us. Mohammed promised me that life would be a paradise. Could they have possibly been lying?

As my eyes begin to focus better through the flames, I can see many people I grew up with who had become martyrs. My grandfathers, several uncles, and my cousins that had all been martyred are all here. I don't understand unless Mohammed and all the imams had been lying to us. I begin to look around, and every imam I knew throughout my short life that had died is here, all here in this miserable place. I begin to look around, and I find the Prophet is here as well. He did not go to a place of paradise like we had been told. He has been here burning in Hell like the rest of us. The stench from all this burning flesh was horrible, but with all the fire and brimstone, no one was burning up.

I began to realize more and more how my own father and mother had lied to me all my life; I realized finally that Mohammed himself had lied to all the people. He really was the evil pariah that the Jews and the Christians had always said that he was. He had led us all by the millions or maybe billions to this awful place of torment. I began to curse him with every part of my being because I didn't want to be in this terrible place. I wanted my palm trees and dates, the flowing streams of cool water, and my 72 virgins that had been promised to me or at least the heaven spoken of by the Christians.

As time passed, I began to realize that there would never be an escape from this place, only misery and as the Christian Bible said, "Wailing and gnashing of teeth." I had finally come to realize that Islam was a religion of Satan and taught nothing but hate. I remembered because, as youngsters, we had to memorize the Koran by the time we were 12 or we would get beaten by the imam and, of course, our fathers. Also, I remembered learning about the ancient gods of Saudi Arabia, the Moon God that was worshiped until Mohammed came along and had his visions from Allah. Somewhere I read that this Moon God traced back to ancient Babylon and Baal worship that had required human blood sacrifices. With all this studying and living our religion, not once in the Koran or the Hadith did I hear or read where the word "love" is mentioned. I wonder why? What was I to do, what could I do? I so desperately want to talk to my mother and younger brothers. I want to warn them about this horrid place and what was awaiting them if they did not repent of their sins and accept Jesus Christ as their Savior. Finally, I realized what a terrible mistake I had made with my life by not taking advantage of all that America had to offer, especially its many churches. I remember listening to some of the preachers on TV. I heard what they were saying, and a few times, I almost fell for their eloquent words. But I had been so well indoctrinated in the Muslim religion that I would not or could not bring myself to believe what they were saying. I listened and scoffed at everything they said.

Now, I am here in the very place that they were preaching against; I had a great opportunity to change my life but didn't take advantage of what Jesus Christ had to offer, so I guess, in a sense, I condemned myself to this torment.

QUESTIONS

12. A MUSLIM SON SPEAKS OUT

There are no questions following this letter. Instead, please pray for the Muslim people that their eyes and hearts may be opened to the Biblical truth of Jesus Christ.

LETTER 13

A FALLEN PASTOR SPEAKS OUT FROM HELL

One former pastor is complaining to the others gathered around him that this just isn't fair that he of all people is in this place of extreme torment with all these sinners:

They deserve to be here, but I certainly don't. I went to the best seminary in my denomination and graduated near the very top of my class. I was married and had two small children when I was hired by a rather large church in a small southern town to be the youth minister and associate pastor. The church had about 1500 active members, so I was on my way to making my mark in the world. About the 3rd year, the senior pastor retired, and I became the senior pastor. Wow, I was barely 35 years old and was now leading a major church in our moderately sized town. After a few years, I decided, without any special education or training, that I would also become a "pastoral counselor." Things worked out fine for a while until one day, a woman came into my office, begging for help. I was aware of her reputation. She had been married at least three times and had slept with almost anyone in town that would have her. She had a tale of woe about her latest husband kicking her out of the house because of her infidelity. I listened intently as she laid out her entire life before me. I was fascinated and began counseling her several times a week. Within a month, I ended up in bed with this woman, and after a few months of seeing her on the side, I left my wife and children to shack up with this evil woman.

In all fairness, I had a beautiful and devoted wife, one who was a schoolteacher as well as the church pianist and organist on Sunday. Also, she pitched in and taught Sunday school if a substitute was needed. Our two children were a true blessing from God, well behaved, and very knowledge-able about the Bible for their young age, thanks to their mother.

After leaving my wife and children for this other woman, the church fired me, and then the denomination revoked my credentials to preach in any of their churches. I didn't bother to repent of my sins with this woman. Instead, I married her after my wife had divorced me. I was sure that God would straighten my new wife out and that we would be able to live happily. I thought I could eventually change to another denomination and get a church. No such luck; within three months of marriage, I caught my new wife in bed with another man. Like her previous three husbands, I threw her out and filed for divorce.

The only jobs that I could get were in several down and out alcohol rehab centers as a counselor. As I repeatedly listened to these derelicts and their lies, I began to hit the bottle myself. After a while, the drinking at night wasn't enough to get me through the miserable days. I began to hide liquor in a thermos jug that supposedly held coffee from home. Of course, I got caught while drunk on the job, and they fired me. Over the next year or two, I moved from one rehab center to another, always getting caught drinking on the job and getting fired. I was humiliated and all alone and saw only one way out that would solve all my problems.

I would take my own life and go straight to heaven if there was such a place. I had begun to doubt the entirety of the Bible and questioned if there was a higher power called God. That night I parked the car in the garage, closed the door, and left the motor running. It didn't take too long. Not only did I take my own life, but I found myself in the place of torment—a place called Hell. But I was sure God was looking for me because, with my education and background, I certainly didn't deserve to be in this place. Someone must have made a mistake. I kept wondering, "who is laughing at me? Why am I on fire but not burning up? I don't understand." I finally began to realize why I was in this awful place. It occurred to me after some time had passed that I needed more than anything to make amends with my precious children and to my first wife, whom I had so totally wronged and humiliated. But how could I, from this place? I decided to write a letter to them, but how could it get delivered from here? I am so very sorry for the mistakes I made, especially for taking up with that evil woman.

I now realize that Satan sent her my way to destroy me, my family, and especially my ministry. Finally, through the fog in my mind and the torment somehow, I remembered Luke 16:26.

"And beside all this, between you and us, there is a
great gulf fixed: so that they which would pass from
hence to you cannot; neither can they pass to us
that would come from thence."

Then it dawned on me almost like a dream that I had once been saved and was one of God's children, but I had let sin come into my life, and I had turned my back on everything Holy. I had thrown my salvation out the door like so much rubbish. I am in this place because I deserve to be here. I can only hope that my children stay true to the word of God and never come to this place of torment. At first, I wanted to blame the "other" woman, but she wasn't the cause of my downfall; she was only the symptom. My downfall started the day I became the senior pastor of this notable church, and I let pride enter my heart. I had begun thinking that I must be a truly great preacher to have such a huge influence and responsibility at such a young age. My sermons changed from Bible-based to "me, based" they were actually more the kind of talks given after dinner at the Rotary Club or some other service-minded organization.

LETTER 14

FALLEN PREACHER #2

(Fallen preachers or False Prophets? Why many people are turned off by preachers)

Since World War II, there has been a steady decline in church attendance and the overall growth of Bible-based churches but a proliferation of "feel good" sanctuaries across the land. Europe has abandoned Christianity with anger directed at God because of the destruction of two world wars within less than 40 years of each other, leaving millions dead and untold amounts of property destroyed along with the rise of godless Communism. Then we have the television age that began in the early 1950s. Soon after TV began to be available across the country, churches began losing their congregations on Sunday nights to the likes of the Ed Sullivan show or Jackie Gleason. Finally, with fewer people attending Sunday night services, many denominations stopped those services altogether.

However, we did seem to have a proliferation of TV church services come along to fill in the gap; at first, for the elderly and infirm who were unable to attend church services on Sunday mornings, this was a blessing. For a time, almost all local TV station programming on Sunday mornings was devoted to local church services. Then the televangelists took over because they could generate huge sums of money, build gargantuan edifices (churches) to affirm their own egos, and live a lavish lifestyle.

> "For there shall arise false Christ's, and false prophets,
> and shall shew great signs and wonders; insomuch
> that, if it were possible, they shall deceive the very
> elect." Matthew 24:24

(Revelation 13:1-18; 16:13-16; 19:20; Daniel 8:24)

> "And whosoever shall exalt himself shall be abased;
> and he that shall humble himself shall be exalted."
> Matthew 23:12

Next, we will look at the confessions of a former pastor that found himself tormented in the everlasting lake of fire. One such pastor was crying and complaining because he found himself in the lake of fire and torment and couldn't understand why. After all, had he not been a model son while growing up? He never smoked or had so much as a single beer or anything else that would dull his senses. Many of his classmates teased him about being Mr. Goody, Goody, throughout high school. While he was in seminary, he met the most beautiful girl who was very much like him with high morals and a kind heart. As they planned their life together, they determined they would be joint ministers in whatever church would hire him as pastor. The years seemed to be flying by as they were leading a small congregation, they had two children by now, and things were going well for them. They were teaching their flock that "love conquers all" and that we were all God's children no matter how we worshipped. Didn't he create all of us?

One day he decided to have a joint service with several leaders of different faiths to show everyone that "we can all get along even though we might worship a little differently." This service went off without a hitch, and the congregation thought it was wonderful that there was no animosity between the different faiths. Life was good, and he was seeing more and more people come into the church all because of his efforts.

About this time, the denominational board of directors asked him to head up their mission board. It was a very important position, and he accepted with great gratitude. This position fit perfectly with the food bank that he had established, as well as the various other civic organizations to which he now belonged.

Then, one night in his study while working late, he felt the sharp pain in his chest, and everything went dark.

When he awoke, he found himself in torment in a lake of fire and brimstone all about him. There were many other lost souls round about, all in extreme agony. Soon, he began to look back and examine his life, trying to figure out what he was doing in this ghastly place that he had preached against for those many years. Finally, it dawned on him that his entire ministry had been a sham. He had preached love, love, and love, but not the Gospel of Jesus Christ. He had failed to preach repentance of sin and the death and resurrection of Jesus. He had even failed to teach about Jesus's coming again because he had some doubts about that. He had a real problem with the entire book of Revelation.

Finally, he realized that he and all of us are just as guilty of sin as the Jews that shouted "crucify him" or the Roman soldier that thrust the spear into Jesus's side. He also realized that our only hope for salvation was in that very blood that was shed for each of us. When we come to Jesus in true repentance of our sins and make Him Lord and master of our lives, he and he alone can and will save us, for He said:

> *"I go to prepare a place for you that where I am, you might be also."*

This pastor, now in the very torment of Hell, could plainly see what he denied or never really understood while alive. After all, his life had been perfect, always doing the right thing even as a child, never smoking, drinking, and no use of vile language. He went to seminary and was ordained as a minister at a very early age. He had married the right girl and had raised two fine children that went into the ministry. He was highly regarded in the community and by his denomination. What more could he have done?

He began to see God's plan from the beginning. For hundreds of years, the shed blood of goats, lambs or pigeons, were offered on an altar for a covering of sin. Each of these sacrifices had to be perfect and without blemish to be offered to God. Then when God led the children of Israel out of Egypt, he demanded that a perfect lamb be sacrificed, and its blood smeared on the doorposts of the houses so that the angel of death would pass over them. Finally, in God's own time, His Son gave His life as a perfect sacrifice for all of mankind. This was God's gift to us.

At last, the good preacher came to realize that he was in Hell not because Jesus had sent him here but because, in truth, he had never fully accepted Christ's atoning sacrifice for all his sins. He just didn't believe what the Bible said about Heaven or

Hell. Until now, this very moment, his thinking had always been that a truly loving God would never send anyone to a damnable place of torment such as this. How terribly wrong he had been all his life.

Review Of The Problem That Sends Many People To An Everlasting Hell

A. Religion – The bondage of religion sends more people to Hell than anything else.

B. Very Religious – Sitting in Church, participating in all the Church functions might make you very religious but spiritually blind.

C. Sermons – Listening to sermon after sermon but never coming to know Jesus.

D. Bondage of Religion – Never knowing the power of God or the peace of God

E. Set Free – Jesus said,

> *"I have come to set the captive free and whom I set free is free indeed."*

Selling out to Jesus breaks the bondage of religion and truly sets you free.

F. Prison – Jesus can open the door of your prison, the prison of religion.

Belief in Jesus Christ as your Savior is what sets Christianity apart from the world's religions.

Christianity is totally based on Christ and what he did for us at the cross on Calvary; all of the rest of the world's religions are totally satanically inspired and human-made; i.e., Mohammedism, Buddhism, Confucianism, Catholicism, Gnosticism, and many different cults as practiced around the world today.

QUESTIONS

13. AND 14. FALLEN PREACHERS

1. Do you and your family regularly attend church and participate in its activities?

    a. the Father _____ yes _____ no

    b. the Mother _____ yes _____ no

    c. the Children _____ yes _____ no

2. When you are unable to attend the Church service of your choice, do you tune in the Sunday morning local church services?

    a. the Father _____ yes _____ no

    b. the Mother _____ yes _____ no

3. Are you caught up in any of the "feel good" churches that teach, I'm ok-you're ok? Some of these churches never teach that salvation only comes through the shed blood of Jesus Christ.

    a. the Father _____ yes _____ no

    b. the Mother _____ yes _____ no

.

4. What did you learn from reading about the former pastor that found himself in the torment of Hell?

_____

_____

5. Do you believe and accept Jesus' sacrifice on Calvary for the forgiveness of your sins?

Husband _____yes _____no

wife _____yes _____no

LETTER 15

GANGSTER WANNA-BE

There was a fellow about my age in my hometown who was a good friend all through high school. I will call him Rolan (not his real name). Rolan was rather heavy-set all his life. He loved to eat almost as much as he loved to drink. He was well on his way to becoming an alcoholic by the time he was 16 years old, and by then, he was probably 75 pounds overweight. He had a motto that he lived by all the days of his life. It was, "I will drink no less than a fifth of good whiskey each and every day." Rolan also loved his beer.

Finally, the glorious day arrived. He had graduated from high school and was now 18 years old. His mother gave him $500 cash for his graduation gift. Rolan hitch-hiked down to New Orleans. He planned on enjoying as much of the sinful life as possible with $500. He returned home five days later, flat broke but, according to the tales, having had a marvelous time. This all sounded great to all his friends since most of us had never experienced anything remotely close to what he had experienced.

As things usually go after high school, most of us parted ways and went off to college or into the military. The Vietnam war was beginning, and no one wanted to get drafted into the Army, so the Air Force and Navy saw a steady rise in their enlistments. We lost track of one another and went our separate ways.

After ten years had passed, I went back home for a class reunion. It became apparent who was missing, and there were a lot of questions. Where was so-and-so? We would learn that he or she had married and now lived in another state, or some were still going to school pursuing advanced degrees.

I had a chance to ask a preacher, friend, and former classmate, about Rolan. My friend told me to come over to his table and sit down, and he would tell me a sad story of a wasted life. He began speaking about trying to get Rolan to come to church with no success. He said that the last time he invited Rolan to church, Rolan pitched a fit and began cursing him for bothering him with that nonsense. He said he wasn't interested and not to bother him; in fact, he said, "don't talk to me again."

My preacher friend went on to say that he had tried to keep up with him, even after he moved to Miami. He said that Rolan had finally found what he was looking for, and that was an element of the gangster life in the drug underworld. He had started out buying and reselling drugs on the street corners of Miami. Rolan was doing quite well as far as the amount of money that was passing through his hands. Finally, the Cuban drug lord for this area of Miami had decided that Rolan was too much competition and made him an offer that he could not refuse. Join them and sell for them, or he would go for a long swim. Rolan quickly became a foot soldier for a drug gang and was the only Caucasian in the group. He thought that he had finally "arrived." The money was rolling in, and the cops no longer hassled him on the streets.

Several others had now joined us at the table, and we began talking about our different experiences with Rolan while growing up. I learned that his father had been killed in Europe during one of the final battles of WWII. His mother had never remarried and had an excellent high ranking job with the Social Security office. She also had a boyfriend that usually came over on Friday afternoon after work and stayed until Monday morning. There was always a lot of drinking and partying going on around Rolan while he was growing up.

One of Rolan's closest friends told of spending the night with Rolan on several different occasions when his mother and her boyfriend would have a few of their friends over. It usually turned into a drunken wife swapping party that went on all night. This was Rolan's home life.

We began to understand a little better why Rolan would never go to church or Sunday school with any of us. Our preacher friend said that he now understood why Rolan had blasted him with an incoherent string of profanity the last time he had tried to talk to him about his very soul. Rolan had not talked to him since but did know what had happened to him. It seems that Rolan started using the drugs he was selling, and he lost a lot of money to the bookies gambling on horses and football. They were putting intense pressure on him to pay up or else. The only source of money Rolan could find to cover his kind of debt was by stealing from his Cuban drug lord.

Rolan began shortchanging his bosses to the tune of many thousands of dollars. The problem was that he stayed high most of the time and didn't realize that they were now onto him. They knew what was going on with their drugs and money. He was in a vicious circle with no way out. On one side, the bookies were threatening him if he didn't come up with their money, and the drug cartel, on the other hand, threatening him if he didn't return the money he had stolen from them. He had no way out of the trap he had set for himself. Rolan was found on a street corner in a drug-infested neighborhood with a bullet hole in the back of his head. No one was ever charged or seriously questioned about his death. Later I learned that his mother did not claim his body or come to his funeral. He was simply buried in a pauper's grave with only a number on the marker.

Rolan had, in effect, destroyed himself many years before with his attitude about Christ, church, and religion in general. It is no wonder that he found himself in torment that morning after being shot by whom he thought was a good friend. One of his fellow drug curriers had shot him.

Like most of the other lost souls in this place of eternal torment, Rolan began blaming everyone but himself. First, he blamed his mother for the way she raised him and all the drunken parties she had right in front of him for all those years. Then he blamed Milton, her boyfriend, for getting his mother drunk and having his way with her.

Rolan remembered bringing a new bride home a few days after their wedding. When they came into the house, Rolan's mother and Milton, and two other couples were going at it like animals. Rolan's new bride didn't say a word. She just left and had the marriage annulled. His wife couldn't accept this life-style and didn't want any part of Rolan after seeing this. At the time, he didn't blame her.

After some time had passed, Rolan began to see through the fog of his mind that he was responsible for his torment. He had, at an early age, rejected Christ, church, and anything to do with religion. He even remembered cursing out our preacher friend for inviting him to come to church.

Rolan's story in Hell was about like everyone else here. They had lived their lives according to the dictates of a sinful heart with no thought of what was awaiting them on the other side. Most of the people had scoffed at the idea of an ever-lasting hell. Like Rolan, most of the people here wanted no part of church and thought all of those "Bible thumpers" were just full of nonsense and wondered how anyone believed anything coming from them?

QUESTIONS

15. GANGSTER WANNA-BE

1. What do you think caused Rolan to have an attitude about all things religious that he had?

    a. His mother, the way he was raised? _____ yes_____ no

    b. Being raised in a single-parent home?_____ yes_____ no

2. As a youngster, was Rolan given too much freedom to do as he pleased with no concern for others? _____ yes_____ no

3. Are you or do you know someone who is headed down this same path of destruction? _____ yes_____ no

4. Is it you? _____ yes_____ no

5. Do you want off this destructive road you have taken?

    _____ yes_____ no

6. Will you accept Jesus Christ as your Savior and turn your life over to him? _____ yes_____ no

7. If, by some chance, you have answered NO to question # 6. I suggest that you get a Bible and skip forward in this book to the chapter, "WHAT THE BIBLE SAYS ABOUT HELL." Look up and read every single one of the scripture verses and then come back to question # 6 and see if your answer is the same or have you now realized that without Christ, you are doomed.

LETTER 16

MY FRIEND BRAD

Growing up, I had a dear friend that I will call Brad. We started in band together in the 7th grade. Even though we ended up going to different high schools, we remained close friends until I moved to another state to start college and eventually start a business of my own.

I invited Brad to go to Sunday school and church with me many times. He always had an excuse until one day, I was finally able to pin him down. Finally, the truth came out. His mother and father didn't believe any of that "junk" in the Bible, and he was not going to waste his time on a lot of "hocus-pocus." I asked him if he had ever read the Bible. When his grandmother died, he said they cleaned out her house and found 2 or 3 Bibles, which his dad threw out with the rest of the trash. To me, this was heartbreaking news about my friend.

Brad was a good kid, never in trouble at school or home. His only brush with the law was when an overzealous policeman wrote him a ticket for going through a four-way stop sign without stopping. The problem was Brad was riding his bicycle, and where the cop was parked, he couldn't see that Brad had stopped before going forward. He got the case against him dismissed when he showed the judge a picture of the corner, where he was, and where the officer was.

Brad worked part-time as a bag boy at a local supermarket in the affluent section of town. As a result, Brad got to meet some of the "best and most desirable" girls in town. He usually had no trouble getting a first date, but it was rare for him to have a second date. I managed to meet one of the girls he had been crazy about, but she would not go out with him a second time. During our conversation about Brad, I asked her why she would not go out with him again. She sat there for several long minutes before finally speaking. She asked me, "Have you ever seen that boy eat? He is disgusting, and I will never sit across a table from him again. Also, he has no manners and does not know how to treat a girl. He pulled up in front of my house and blew the car horn. Finally, after about 10 minutes, he got out and came to the door. He was angry that I expected him to come inside and meet my parents. He had invited me to dinner at a nice restaurant, so I thought everything would be ok. Wrong. Brad apparently had no idea how to use a knife and fork. He picked up everything with his fingers, including his steak. He just picked it up and bit off a mouthful, and then proceeded to chew and talk at the same time. Gross! For dessert, Brad got pecan pie with ice cream. He did use his spoon to eat the ice cream, but picked up the pie with his fingers and ate it like it was a slice of cornbread."

All that I could say was that I had no idea. The only time we had ever eaten together was at a drive-in where we got sandwiches, basically finger food anyway. She said that she felt sorry for him and didn't understand why his parents had not taught him anything. She suggested that I talk with him, and I promised that I would.

The next day I went to a bookstore and bought a copy of

"Emily Post's book of Etiquette" and gave it to Brad with a suggestion on which chapters might help him get a second date.

A few weeks later, I asked Brad if he had taken any time to read the book I gave him. He looked at me in complete astonishment and said, "I threw that book away; there was nothing in it that I needed to learn."

Brad was always "happy go lucky" in everything that he did. Finally, in his senior year, he met a beautiful girl and had invited her to go to the prom with him the next Saturday night. She agreed, and they went out Friday night before the big date. Everything was finally working out for Brad, a second date, and even to the prom where he could show off this beauty.

Well, as usual, Brad had to work Saturday until about 4:00 pm. He got off early and went home to shower and put on the tux he had rented. He had bought a beautiful orchid corsage for his date. All was right with the world, or so he thought.

Brad got to Ginny's house, went to the door, and rang the bell. Ginny's dad came to the door and, with a look of total bewilderment, asked Brad what he wanted. Brad told him that Ginny and he were going to the prom. Her dad walked out onto the porch and told him to have a seat. He then asked Brad when he had last spoken with Ginny. Brad said, "last night." We went to the movies together."

Ginny's dad then broke the news to Brad that the family had just returned from church. Ginny had gotten married that afternoon at 2:00 and was now on her honeymoon. Brad was devastated for several days and took to drinking heavily.

I never saw Brad again after moving out of state the next year, but I did keep up with him as well as I could. The last I heard of him was probably in 1967 0r '68. He had gotten married. His wife had given birth to a little boy, and everyone that knew Brad said that he almost worshipped his wife and their little boy.

Then something happened, and no one knew exactly what took place. It was rumored that Brad's wife's grandmother had died. Brad wouldn't go with her to the funeral, and when she returned home, she brought her grandmother's Bible with her, which had marriage death and birth records going back to the early 1800s recorded.

The next day Brad's wife returned to work, and in her absence, Brad threw the grandmother's Bible in the garbage. He also went through her lingerie drawers and found two more Bibles, which he threw away. Brad's wife left him that week and filed for divorce. Everyone said that he was absolutely devastated.

The day the divorce was final, Brad drank rat poison along with a half-bottle of whiskey and took his own life. What a horrible death that must have been.

BRAD FINALLY AWOKE TO A SMELL HE DID NOT RECOGNIZE UNTIL HE realized that he smelled his own flesh burning. The puzzling thing to him was that though he was on fire and he could smell his flesh burning, it wasn't turning to ashes or anything else; it was just burning. As the smoke cleared, he looked around. There standing in front of him, was his father. Brad cursed him for betraying him as a child and not leading him to a saving knowledge of Jesus Christ. Everything that he had heard about church, religion, and especially Jesus was now very real to him. Oh, if he only had his life to live over again, he would make many changes in his own being. He would go to Sunday school and church with his friends when they invited him.

Once again, he approached his father, asking him, "why,

dad? Why? I didn't have to die and come to this place. My wife left me and took our son because I refused to go to church with her, and, following your example, I threw out her Bible and forbade her to bring another into our home. I refused to let her take my son to pre-school at a church. I was totally against everything holy, and now, following in your footsteps, I doomed myself. Dad, in truth, I really can't blame you. I can only blame myself."

QUESTIONS

16. MY FRIEND BRAD

1. Why do you think Brad turned out the way he did? Did his parents spend too much time working to attend to the needs of a young child? _____ yes_____ no

2. Did you have the same kind of parents, or do you know someone that does? _____ yes_____ no

3. Brad was left to raise himself with little to no parental supervision or guidance. Are you or do you know of someone like that? _____ yes_____ no

4. If you answered yes, what are you going to do about it?
   (Check all that apply)
   a. Talk to the parents?____
   b. Talk to and try to help your friend?____
   c. Reach out in Christian love to help?____
   d. Do nothing and hope for the best?____

5. Try to witness to your friend and win him/her to Christ?

_____ yes_____ no

LETTER 17

A STORY ABOUT TIMMY, MY NEIGHBOR

Timmy was a lad born to a rather affluent couple that really had no interest in having a family. As his mother would say to her friends, "Timmy was an "oops," he was not supposed to have been."

As Timmy became a teenager, it was evident that he was a little different from other boys his age. He had not gone through puberty with the usual facial hair (whiskers) or arm and leg hair. Also, his voice had not changed that much. As time went by, Timmy let his hair grow out in long waves, very similar to his older girl cousins. At about 14 or 15 years, he began to have his eyebrows arched. When his cousin made him up and dressed him, he was quite effeminate or, as some might say, rather pretty. He looked much more like a girl than a young boy.

Now, let's take a moment and see what the Bible has to say about Timmy's girlie tendency.

"Know ye not that the unrighteous shall not inherit the Kingdom of God? Be not Deceived: neither fornicators, nor idolaters, nor adulterers, nor effeminate or abusers of themselves with mankind. "1st Corinthians 6:9

June 26, 2015, was probably one of the most devastating days in the history of our country caused by the Supreme Court of the United States. In a case known to the court as *Obergefell v. Hodges, the Supreme court held that "the right to marry is a fundamental right inherent in the liberty of the person, and under the Due Process and Equal Protection Clauses of the Fourteenth Amendment couples of the same sex may not be deprived of that right and liberty."* This ruling dealt a devastating blow to those of us who believe the Bible and its definition of marriage as a monogamous, heterosexual union between one man and one woman as ordained by God.

What has been even more disastrous is that many mainstream denominations have wholeheartedly accepted this disgrace. Some have also jumped the gun and started approval of homosexual marriage, such as the Presbyterian Church (USA). They voted to recognize "same-sex marriage" as a union of 'two people and not just a man and woman.

Some might think that we are picking on the gay population, but this sin is contrary to nature and rubs against God's created order. Three times in Romans 1, Paul emphasizes that homosexual sin is contrary to nature or is unnatural. "And likewise also the men, leaving the natural use of the woman, burned in their lust one toward another; men with men working that which is unseemly, and receiving in themselves that recompense of their error which is meet. In this one verse, homosexuality is called unnatural, indecent, error, and bringing a due penalty." Romans 1:27

In the '60s and '70s, people of all walks of life considered same-sex sexual intimacy wrong. In the last twenty or so years, the steady avalanche that has culminated in the legality of same-sex marriage has been nothing short of breathtaking and obviously designed by Satan.

Turning to God's word, four main biblical passages refer negatively to the issue of homosexual activity:

1. The story of Sodom (Genesis 19:1-13)

2. The Levitical texts (Leviticus 18:22; 20:13)

3. Paul's description of a society fallen away from God (Romans 1:26-32)

4. Two lists by Paul, each containing a reference to homosexual practice of some kind (1st Corinthians 6:9-10 and 1st Timothy 1:8-11)

The Genesis 19 passage refers to the homosexual desires of the men of Sodom toward the two male visitors who were angels in human form.

Romans 1:26-32 says,

> *"God gave them over to degrading passions; for their*
> *women exchanged the natural function for that*
> *which is unnatural, and in the same way also the*
> *men abandoned the natural function of the woman*
> *and burned in their desire toward one another, men*
> *with men committing indecent acts and receiving*
> *in their own persons the due penalty of their error.*
> *"*

1stCorinthians 6:9-10 is an ugly list of sins that are incompatible with the Kingdom of God and the Gospel –

> *"or do you not know that the unrighteous will not*
> *inherit the Kingdom of God? Do not be deceived;*
> *neither fornicators, nor idolaters, nor adulterers,*

nor effeminate [homosexuals], *nor thieves, nor the*
covetous, nor drunkards, nor revilers, nor
swindlers, will inherit the Kingdom of God."

Two of the Greek words used:

Malakos sometimes translated "effeminate," means "soft to the touch." Among the Greeks, it referred to males who assumed the passive role in homosexual intercourse."

Arsenokoitai' found in 1st Corinthians 6:9, is a Compound of arsen (man) and koite (bed). An accurate Translation is "bedder of man," or someone who takes Men to bed. The clear meaning is men engaged in homo-sexual activity. Paul was probably referring to Leviticus 18:22 and 20:13. The Leviticus passages called for the death penalty for homosexual intercourse and called it an "abomination."

1st John 2:16 tells us –

> *"For all that is in the world, the lust of the flesh, and*
> *the lust of the eyes, and the pride of life, is not of*
> *the Father, but it is of the world. Its temptations to*
> *the believer are twofold: lust for the sensual and*
> *pride in the mastery of his own life."*

NOW, BACK TO LITTLE TIMMY, THE EFFEMINATE KID. TIMMY HAD reached middle school and was required to take a physical education class with the other boys in his class. The one thing that became apparent to Timmy almost immediately was that after an hour of physical activity, all the boys had to shower together in open showers with a total lack of privacy. At first, Timmy was self-conscious, but this soon gave way to curiosity, seeing all these other naked boys thrilled him.

He began to have feelings that he had never known before and could think of nothing else, day and night.

It wasn't long before Timmy couldn't control himself and began trying to find another boy with similar feelings and desires. It happened after school one day as he was walking home. Another boy that he had noticed several times in the communal shower stopped him and invited him to come up to his apartment; his parents wouldn't be home for several hours. Timmy was both nervous and excited about the possibility of his first encounter with another boy.

They went into the boy's bedroom and immediately got undressed.

Later as Timmy was walking on toward his own home, he was thinking about the wonderful time he had had with his first homosexual experience.

Over the next several months, until school was out for the summer, Timmy and his friend met almost every day. Soon these one-on-one encounters were not enough to satisfy Timmy. He began to sneak out of the house and go around town to the "gay" bars and dives. He had quickly evolved into the "lifestyle." By the time Timmy was a senior in high school, he had been with dozens of different boys and men, some old enough to have been his father and possibly his grandfather.

Timmy was now a full-blown homosexual and didn't care who knew it. When he went out prowling for new conquests, he would sometimes dress as a girl, and he quickly found that a lot of men would pay him quite well just to be with him.

One night he came home later than usual, and there was his mother and her estranged husband sitting in his room waiting for him. Timmy was caught off guard and surprised to learn that his parents had figured out what he was doing and what he had become. They told him to pack a bag, to get out, and never come back because he no longer had a home. Timmy slept in his car that night and gave a lot of thought as to what he would or could do. He had heard about the "gay bath-houses" in San Francisco. He decided that he would go there and probably make a lot of money.

It took Timmy a few days to get to the Bay area. He found the district that had several bathhouses. In his sick mind, he thought to himself, "I have finally arrived." After a few days of learning the ropes to this new lifestyle, Timmy began to fit right in. He started taking in a lot of money, especially from the real perverts, but that was ok with him if they had the money.

Timmy lived this lifestyle for several years and could still pass himself off as a girl most of the time. Times were good, or so he thought. One afternoon, a little after 4:00 pm, a young, well-dressed man came in and took up with him. This guy told Timmy that he was married and had two daughters and another on the way. He was from another large mid-western city and was in town for the week. He bought Timmy for the next five days, and Timmy satisfied his every need or want. Then he was gone.

Several months passed, Timmy had forgotten all about this paying customer. That was how Timmy looked at all the "nice boys" now, just paying customers. Timmy was sitting at the bar, enjoying a refreshing drink, when this guy sat down beside him and said, "Do you remember me?" Timmy vaguely remembered him but denied knowing him. The guy then started to curse Timmy and shouted out where everyone in the place could hear him and said, "You gave me AIDs, and in turn, I gave it to my wife and our newborn baby!" With that statement, he stood up behind Timmy and shot him twice in the back of his head; he then turned the gun on himself and took his own life.

Unfortunately for Timmy, this was not the end of every-thing. He found himself swirling around in a black tunnel like he had seen depicted in movies. As he fell farther and farther, he kept hearing evil laughter and screams that kept getting louder and louder. Finally, he stopped swirling around and around and could see many other people all around him. All of them seemed to be in some sort of excruciating pain and torment. The flames began to lick at his feet and worked their way up his entire body to the point that he was totally engulfed, but for some reason that he did not understand, he was not burning up like a piece of firewood.

Timmy cried out in anguish, "where am I? What is happening to me?" Suddenly an evil looking being appeared in front of him and, laughing at his discomfort, told him that he was in hell and would be here forever and ever. This being was then joined by several more with his same countenance, and they all teased and made fun of him. One of the beings said to him, "Why don't you call on your Jesus to help you?"

Timmy quite innocently said, "Who is he? I never heard of him?" "Can he really help?" With that, the evil beings left Timmy alone in his torment.

QUESTIONS

#17. A STORY ABOUT TIMMY, MY NEIGHBOR

1. Do you know of someone that is like Timmy?

Yes _____ No _____

2. Are you like Timmy, or do you have these tendencies?

Yes _____ No _____

3. Will you give Christian witness backed by sound Biblical scriptures to try to win this person to Christ? Gently explaining that Christ can and will set him free and forgive him of his sin.

Yes _____ No _____

LETTER 18

GOD ANSWERS PRAYER

This event was told from a pulpit of a sizeable Charismatic Church by a well-known TV-evangelist that met this man several years after this incident took place.

There was a famous movie producer that had finished filming a movie down in south Alabama. There was the usual after-work drunken party with the cast and the general debauchery that goes on. He woke up several days later in a small motel room and could not remember how he got there.

Sitting there on the side of the bed, he began to reflect on his life and take stock of where he was. He decided that he need to get back to Hollywood as soon as possible, so he looked at a map and decided that the fastest route would be through south Alabama down to I-10 and straight across the country. As he traveled these back roads through one small town after another, he saw the abject poverty in which some of these people lived. On many of the small-town main streets, a number of the buildings were boarded up and had fallen into disrepair. The more he saw, the more dejected he became.

After a while, he had decided that he was going to end his

life because he saw himself as a complete failure. Two failed marriages and the third one filing for divorce, four children that wouldn't talk to him. What did he have to live for? He was looking for a secluded spot to pull over and end his life when he spotted a sign:

Sunbeam Worship Center
ALL ARE WELCOME
1 mile on the left.

He thought to himself that it might be a good idea to check this out. Maybe I can slip in the back door and sit on a back pew unnoticed and say a few "Hail Mary's and a few Our Fathers." When he pulled into the parking lot, he was surprised to find a dozen or so cars there. He parked and went inside and quietly sat down on a back-row as planned. The sanctuary was dark except down front, right in front of the Alter. That area lit up by a beam of sunlight streaming through a window. About a dozen or so ladies were sitting in a circle. It must have been some type of strange cult because he heard languages he had never heard before, and he had been all over the world.

Suddenly a little old grey-haired lady noticed him and came back to where he was sitting. She asked him if she could help him or if he needed anything, was he hungry? They had plenty of food. He assured her that he wasn't hungry but appreciated her kind offer.

She sat next to him for a few minutes in silence, and finally, she reached over and took his hand in hers. She said, "I know something very important is on your mind; I can tell just by looking at you. You are struggling with some problem, and you haven't quite decided what to do. Let me, no, let us help you; come with me." She led him down front to where the other ladies were sitting in a circle. She told the other ladies that this was Mr. Stranger because she had not asked for his name, so they all decided just to call him Mr. Stranger. He was ok with that; he thought for sure he had fallen into some cult of strange people.

The leader of the group stood up and lifted her hands toward heaven, and began speaking in this strange language again. He was now about ready to run out the door, but something held him back. After a few moments, another lady stood up and, in plain English, said that what the first strange talking lady had said was that this gentleman was demonically possessed, and they needed to get rid of his demons before he could be saved.

He was thinking, "Saved from what?" About this time, the leader slapped her hand onto his forehead and began to pray in that strange language again. After a few minutes, several more of the women placed their hands on his head, and suddenly like a clap of thunder, he felt a jolt in his body, almost like an electric shock. It seemed to happen dozens of times as these kindly ladies prayed for him. They explained to him later that he had these sensations as the demons were leaving his body.

After a while, they stopped praying and began to ask him a lot of questions about his life and why he had picked their small church? He told them that he had decided earlier that day that he was going to end his miserable life, and by accident, he had spotted their church. He came in and sat down on the back pew and would have left if the lady hadn't come back to him and led him to the front.

Something miraculously had happened in the short time he had been here. For the first time in, he didn't know how many years he felt free, and he did begin to realize that perhaps there was something to this demon stuff mentioned in the Bible.

He told them that he was on his third marriage and she had kicked him out of the house and that none of his four children would speak to him. This lady's prayer circle listened and began to pray and lay hands on him once more. Finally, he broke down in tears and asked Jesus to come into his heart and give him what these dear ladies had and that more than anything, he wanted to be saved. As was suggested, he began to confess a lifetime of sins and begged God to forgive him. One of the ladies went back into the church office and brought a Bible out to him and gave it to him. She said, "Usually, the pastor gives a Bible to everyone who makes a profession of faith in Jesus Christ, and I know he would want you to have one." He accepted the gift with much gratitude and left to go back home to Hollywood.

He spent the next three days on the road driving, thinking, and praising God for the miracle that had happened in his life. On the way back home, he decided that he could no longer live in the apartment he had rented because there had been too much sin in that place. When he arrived home, he asked the apartment manager to retrieve some papers that he needed and told him that he could have everything there. He didn't want any of it, and he paid him for the remainder of the year's rent.

After that, he looked up a small church of the same denomination as the one in south Alabama, and had a long talk with the pastor and told him all about what had taken place at the Sunbeam Worship Center with the lady's prayer circle. The preacher understood precisely what had happened to him and why. He then suggested that he go over and try to patch things up with his wife because he was a changed man from what she remembered of him.

He took his time driving across town to their mega-mansion, but he slowly made his way to the front door and rang the bell. He almost turned and ran away several times, but something was pulling him forward and telling him to stay.

His wife finally opened the door and had a bewildered look

on her face the minute he spoke to her. She had not seen or heard from him in almost three years, and she was shocked to see how much his countenance had changed. There was virtually a glow about him and a new sparkle in his eyes, and something else was quite different. He was standing there holding a Bible in his hand and was dressed differently from anything she remembered about him.

He finally got the words out that he would like to come in and talk to her, but if she didn't want to talk, he would understand and would just leave.

She was intrigued and wanted to know more about the changes she was seeing. She invited him in and offered to fix him a drink. He refused and told her that he no longer drank alcohol in any form and no longer smoked those smelly cigars. She was dumbfounded and asked what had happened to him that had caused him to make so many changes in his life.

He began telling her the story about how he had decided to end his life but somehow had been led to the Sunbeam Worship Center down in south Alabama. He related how the lady's prayer circle had prayed with and for him and had cast out many demons that were controlling his miserable life. He told her of hearing these ladies speaking in strange languages and how he had also begun speaking in "tongues," as the Pentecostals called it. He said that they had told him that he had been baptized in the Holy Spirit, and the evidence was speaking in tongues.

After several hours of conversation, he finally got up enough courage to ask her if he could come home. She immediately threw her arms around him and said that was something she had been praying for ever since he left. She suggested that they talk to a minister over at the Cathedral.

He told her he had already found a true Bible-believing Pentecostal church similar to the one in south Alabama, and the minister was expecting them. She agreed, and they went to see him. They decided to both join the church the next Sunday morning. The minister said that he would hold a special baptism for them after the regular service.

The minister finished his sermon and gave an invitation for anyone wanting to be saved and join the church to please come forward as the choir began to sing. The couple slipped out of their pew and made their way to the front of the church. A little while later, the pastor told the congregation that he was going to break precedent and have a special baptism for our newest members today. He led them into a chamber behind the choir loft and told them to go to the dressing room and put on the white robes that were waiting laid out for them and that one of the elders would be waiting to escort them to the baptismal pool.

The pastor was waiting for them and baptized the gentleman first and then his wife. Afterward, he told them to get dressed and come back into the auditorium to be received by the congregation and that there was a surprise awaiting them.

The couple did as they were told and quickly changed and came back into the auditorium, where the congregation was waiting to greet them as the newest members. There stood three of the children that had not spoken to their father in over five years. The other son was in the army and unable to be there.

There was a lot of hugging and tears, not only in the family but all over the church. Everyone in the congregation now knew who this special man was. Some had even heard the story of his experience at the Sunbeam Worship Center in Alabama.

Later that night, he sat down and wrote a rather lengthy letter to the Ladies Prayer Circle at the little south Alabama church and enclosed a check for $10,000.00 as an appreciation gift for them literally saving his life. Of course, he told them of reuniting with his family, his baptism, and his wife's. He also explained how his children had come to this "miraculous" event.

A few weeks later, his new pastor came to the house and asked him if he would be willing to go with him to a church conference and tell his story to a church leadership group. He said that he thought his story of God's mercy and saving grace would be very inspirational to many of their denomination's leaders.

From this one talk, he began speaking at meetings and conferences all over the country, not just in his denomination. He gave credit to the lady's prayer circle at the Sunshine Worship Center down in South Alabama each and every time he spoke.

QUESTIONS

#18. GOD ANSWERS PRAYER

Unlike the previous stories, this one has a happy ending; therefore, only two comparative questions will be asked.

These may be the most important question you will ever be asked, and God forbid that this becomes true for you today.

If, by chance, you drew your last breath today and found yourself standing before Jesus at his seat of judgment, what would He say to you?

1. Would it be, enter paradise, you good and faithful servant?

_____ yes_____ no

2. Or, would Jesus look at you and say, "depart from me, you wicked servant, I never knew you?" _____ yes_____ no

If you answered <u>Yes </u>to question # 1 and <u>No</u> to question # 2, then you are on the right road. Jesus said that the road that leads to destruction is broad and many are on it, but the road that leads to life is narrow, and few will find it.

PART II

THE BIBLE

REFERENCES

WHAT THE BIBLE SAYS ABOUT HELL

(a partial listing from)
DAKE'S ANNOTATED REFERENCE BIBLE, KING JAMES
Version
(Printed here with permission)

2nd Samuel 22:6 the (i) sorrows of hell compassed me about; (j) the snares of death prevented me.

n. I Heb. chebel, cords, throes, pains, pangs, sorrows – of hell (Heb. sheol, the unseen world.

These compassed him about.) n. j the snares (Heb. moqesh, nooses, hooks, snares, or traps) of death preceded me. They were in my path that I should fall into them and die; but the Lord heard me, and I was snatched out of them in due time. Job 11:8 It is as (c) high as heaven; what canst thou do? Deeper than (d) hell; what canst thou know?

n. c the height of heaven is here contrasted with the depth of sheol, this identifies heaven as above the other infinite heights of creation and hell as in the lowest parts of the earth beneath. The hell beneath could not possibly be the grave on the surface of the earth. n. d Heb. sheol the place of departed spirits, not the grave, the place of the body. Psalm 9:17 (i) The wicked shall be turned into (j) hell, and all (k) the nations that forgot God. n. i 5th prophecy in Psalms (9:17-18, partially fulfilled and will be completed when the last of the wicked are in hell and the righteous are vindicated and safe with God forever.

n. j Where are the dead?

That hell is the grave is one of the most popular themes of all false cults. They, without exception, change the Bible to suit themselves and gain converts who are always glad to accept any method of escape from the reality of hell. Their tactics remind one of the free translations of the new electronic brain designed to translate English into Russian. It was fed the words, "The spirit is willing, but the flesh is weak." The machine answered with a sentence in Russian, "The whiskey is agreeable, but the meat has gone bad.

Where is the harmony between the two statements? To make hell the grave and the grave Hell is just as ridiculous, for different Hebrew and Greek words are used for hell and grave.

These are two distinct subjects and a foreign to each other as heaven is to hell. There is no possible harmony of scripture when we force the same meaning for hell and the grave.

(See notes on Hell and Resurrection of the Dead)

n. k Why should the wicked and all the nations that forgot God be turned into hell if hell is a grave? Do not the righteous also go to the grave at death?

Hell. The English word hell is defined in our dictionaries as "the abode of evil spirits; the infernal regions; place of eternal punishment or extreme torment; in ancient times, the place of departed spirits. The word infernal means "belonging to hell. The word inferno is another word for "the infernal regions; hell." Gehenna is defined as "the place of future torment; hell:

hellfire." Tartarus is defined as "the place of punishment in the lower world."

There are 7 Hebrew and Greek words translated hell and grave as follows:

Hebrew – sheol, the unseen world. It always refers to the unseen world of departed spirits, and Is always in contrast with the Hebrew geber, which means the grave, or the seen world where Bodies are buried. Oeber is always translated grave, burying place, sepulcher. It is never translated hell, and this is correct. Sheol is translated hell 31 times (Deut. 32:22; 2nd Sam. 22:6; Job 11:8; 26:6; Ps. 9:17; 16:10; 18:5; 55:15; 86:13; 116:3; 139:8; Pr. 5:5; 7:27; 9:18; 15:11; 24:23; 14:27; Isa. 5:14; 14:9; 15:28; 15:18; 57:9; Ezek. 31:16-17; 32:21; 27:; Amos 9:2; Jonah 2:2; Hab. 2:5) Sheol is translated grave 31 times (Gen. 37:35; 42:38; 44:29, 31; 1st Sam. 2:6; 1st Ki. 2:6, 9; Job 7:9; 14:13; 17:13; 21:13;24:19; Ps. 6:5; 30:3; 31:17; 49:14-15; 88:3; 89:48; 141:7; Pr. 1:12; 30:16; Eccl. 9:10; Isa. 14:11; 38:10, 18; Ezek. 31:15; Hos. 13:14) Sheol is translated pit 3 times (Num. 16:30, 33; Job 17:16) Hebrew geber the proper word for grave, the seen world is translated 6 different ways and always of the place where the body goes at death.

(1) Grave (Gen. 35:20; 50:5; Num. 19:16; 18:2; 2nd Sam. 3:32; 19:37; 1st Kin. 13:30; 14:13; 2ndKin. 22:20; 2nd Chr. 34:28; Job 3:22; 5:26; 10:19; 21:32; Ps. 88:5, 11; Isa. 14:19; 53:9; Ezek. 32:23-24; Nah. 1:14) (2) Graves (Ex. 14:11; 2nd Ki. 23:6; 2nd Chr. 34:4; Job 17:1; Isa. 65:4; Jer. 8:1; Ezek. 32:22-25; 37:12-13; 39:11)

(3) Burial (2nd Chronicles 26:23; Ecclesiastes 6:3; Isiah 14:20; Jeremiah 22:19)

(4) Burying place (Genesis 23:4, 9, 20, 47:30; 50:13; Judges 16:31)

(5) Sepulcher (Genesis 23:6; Deuteronomy 34:6; Judges 8:32; 1st Samuel 10:2; 2nd Samuel 2:32; 4:12; 17:23; 21:14; 1st Kings 13:22, 31; 2nd Kings 9:28; 13:21; 21:26.

23:17, 30; Psalms 5:9; Isiah 22:16; Jeremiah 5:16)

(6) Sepulchers (Genesis 23:6; 2nd Kings 23:16; 2nd Chronicles 16:14; 21:20; 24:25; 28:27.

32:33; 35:24; Nehemiah 2:3' 5; 3:16)

Hades (Greek) the unseen world. It is equivalent to sheol of the Old Testament and is always in Contrast with mnaymion, the seen world, or place of bodies at death.

Mnaymion meaning the grave is never translated hell.

Hades is translated grave 1 time in (1st Corinthians 15:55)

Mnaymion (Greek) the proper word for grave is translated 6 different ways as follows:

(1) Grave (John 11:17, 31, 38; 12:17)

(2) Graves (Matthew 27:52-53; Luke 11:44; John 5:28; Revelation 11:9)

(3) Tomb (Matthew 27:60; Mark 6:29)

(4) Tombs Matthew 8:28; Mark 5:2-5; Luke 8:27)

(5) Sepulcher (Matthew 27:60; 28:8; Mark 15:46; 16:2-8; Luke 23:53, 55; 24:1-2, 9, 12, 22, 24; John 19:41-42; 20:1-11; Acts 2:29; 7:16; 13:29)

(6) Sepulchers (Matthew 23:29; Luke 11:47-48) Gehenna (Greek) from Hebrew gay, gorge or valley, and Hinnom, a Jebusite name. It means valley of Hinnom, where perpetual fires burn the refuse of Jerusalem. It came to be used by the Jews as an appropriate picture of eternal hell and eternal punishment.

Gehenna is translated 12 times (Matthew 5:22, 29, 30; 10:28; 18:9 23:15, 33; Mark 9:43-47; Luke 12:5; James 3:6) It is never translated grave and this is correct. (see Luke 5:12)

Tartaroo (Greek); Tartarus (Latin) the deepest abyss of sheol-hades, the unseen world. (see 2nd Pet. 2:4)

Adamite rebels against God. It is used 5 times (Revelation 19:20; 20:10-15; 21:8)

It can be seen from a study of all the above scriptures on sheol-hades. Gehenna, Tartarus, and geber-mnaymion that hell is not the grave, but a place of consciousness and torment. This will be abundantly proved in the following facts about hell and the grave:

FACTS PROVING HELL NOT THE GRAVE:

(1) In Scripture, sheol-hades (hell) is never the place of the body: geber-mnaymion (grave) never the place of the soul. (Psalms 16:10; Acts 2:25-29)

(2) Sheol never is plural; geber is plural 38 times; singular 74 times.

(3) Sheol never located on earth; geber located on earth 73 times.

(4) Body never goes to sheol; body mentioned as going to geber 75 times.

(5) Individual's sheol never mentioned; individual's Gebers mentioned 79 times.

(6) Man, never puts anyone in sheol; man puts bodies into Gebers 40 times.

(7) Man, never digs or makes a sheol; man digs or makes Gebers 51 times.

(8) Man, on earth never touches a sheol; he touches Gebers 51 times.

(9) Man has never seen a sheol on earth; he has seen Gebers 51 times.

(10) God alone puts men into sheol (Numbers 16:30-33; 1st Samuel 2:6; Ezekiel 31:16.

(11) God alone will bring men out of sheol (1st Samuel 2:6; Revelation 20:11-15)

(12) Hell-bound men descend (Isiah 5:14) and go down (into lower part of the earth) into Sheol at death (Genesis 37:35; 42:38; 44:29, 31; Numbers 16:30-33; 17:16; 21:13.

1st Samuel 2:6; 1st Kings 2:6, 9; Job 7:9-10; 17:16; 21:13;

Psalms 31:16-17; Isiah 14:9-16; Ezekiel 31:15-17; 32:27; Matthew 11:23; Luke 16:10-15)

(13) Men go into sheol in a moment and quickly (Numbers 16:30-33; Job 21:13; Psalms 55:15; Luke 16:19-31)

(14) Men are forced into sheol (Isiah 5:15)

(15) Men are cast into sheol (Ezekiel 31:15-17)

(16) Sheol is located in the nether parts of the earth (Ezekiel 31:14-18; 32:24) lower parts of the earth (Psalms 63:9; 68:18; Ephesians 4:8-10), heart of the earth (Matthew 12:40) below the depth of the seas and below the foundations of the mountains (Jonah 2:2-6;) beneath like a pit (Proverbs 15:24; Isiah 14:9-16; Ezekiel 31:14-18; 32:18-31; and is too deep to dig into (Job 11:8; Amos 9:2)

(17) Sheol-hades, unlike the grave, is a place of activity, a place of wrath (Deuteronomy 32:22; Luke 16:19-31) (18) A place of sorrow (Genesis 42:38; 44:29, 31; 2nd Samuel 22:6; Psalms 18:5; 55:15; 116:3; Proverbs 7:27; Isiah 14:9-15)

(19) A place of fire (Deuteronomy 32:22; Luke 16:19-31)

(20) A place hidden from man, but naked before God (Job 26:6; Proverbs 15:11; Psalms 139:8; Amos 9:20

(21) A place of power (Psalms 49:15; Hosea 13:14; Matthew 16:18; 1st Corinthians 15:51-56; Revelation 1:18; 6:8)

(22) A place of full consciousness (Isiah 14:9-15; Ezekiel 32:27-31; Luke 16:19-31)

(23) A place for the soul and spirit, not the body (Psalms 16:10; 30:3; 49:15; 86:13; 89:48; Proverbs 23:14; Acts 2:25-29

(24) A place of conversations (Isiah 14:9-16; Ezekiel 32:21; Luke 16:19-31)

(25) A place where many kings and chief ones of the earth live after death (Isiah 14:9-11)

MORTALITY OF THE BODY

The body is now mortal. It will die and go back to dust (Genesis 3:19; Ecclesiastes3:19-21; Hebrews 9:27.

James 2:26) This procedure will continue until sin is put down and death is destroyed (1st Corinthians 15:24-28.

Revelation 21:3-7; 22:3)

RESURRECTION OF THE DEAD

This refers only to the bodies of all men who die, not to the souls and spirits, which are immortal. All scripture on the future resurrection of the dead, without exception, refer only to the bodies which die and will be resurrected from dust again (Daniel 12:2; John 5:28-29; 1st Corinthians 15; 1st Thessalonians 4:13-17. Revelations 20:4-6, 11-15). There will be no spiritual resurrection - a resurrection of the soul and spirit. All spiritual resurrection is accomplished in this life before the body dies (Ephesians 2:1-10; Colossians 2:11-13).

If one is not resurrected spiritually from death in trespasses and sins in this life, he will remain forever spiritually dead or separated from God (Hebrews9:27; Revelation 22:11)

NO SOUL-SLEEP TAUGHT IN SCRIPTURE

All scripture used by false cults to prove soul-sleep really refer to death of the body which knows nothing in the grave.

IMMORTALITY OF THE BODY

The body, which is now mortal, will become immortal in the resurrection. All scriptures mentioning future immortality refer to the body, not to the soul, which is now immortal.

THE INTERMEDIATE STATE

By this, it means the state of the dead between death and the resurrection of the body. After the body goes back to dust at physical death (Genesis 3:19; Ecclesiastes 3:19-21; James 2:26), It remains dead (separated from the inner man) until the future resurrection day when the body will be made immortal (1st Corinthians 15:35-54). The soul and spirit continue alive, being immortal either in heaven or hell, until the resurrection day when the body will be made immortal. At physical death, the soul and spirit leave the body (James 2:26). If one is a converted person his soul and spirit go up to heaven immediately at death to await the resurrection of the body (Luke 20:38; John 11: 25-26; 2nd Corinthians 5:8; Ephesians 3:15; 4:8-10; Philemon 1:21-24; Hebrews 12:22-23; Revelation 6:9-11). If he is a sinner his soul and spirit go to hell at death to await the resurrection of the body (Luke 16:19-31; 2nd Peter 2:9; Revelation 20:11-15; Isiah 14:9)

REVELATION 20:10-14

10. And the devil that deceived them was cast into the lake of fire and brimstone where the beast and the false prophet are and shall be tormented day and night for ever and ever. (The beast and the false prophet were cast into the lake of fire 1,000 years before this (v. 19:20. They are still there after 1,000 years proving that hell and eternal torment are realities. If one cannot burn up in 1,000 years he will never do so (Revelation 14:9-11; Matthew 25:46; Isiah 66:22-24).

11. And I saw a great white throne, and him that sat on it, from whose face the earth and the heaven fled away; and there was found no place for them.

12. And I saw the dead, small and great, stand before God;

and the books were opened: and another book was opened; which is *the book* of life; and the dead were judged out of those things which were written in the books <u>according to their works</u>.

13. And the sea gave up the dead which were in it; and <u>death and hell</u> delivered up the dead which were in them; and they were judged every man according to their works.

14. And death and hell were cast into the lake of fire. This is the second death.

15. And <u>whosoever</u> was not found written in the book of life was cast into the lake of fire.

EPILOGUE

A few years ago, a short video came across my computer that I kept for several years and finally lost it with one of the many Windows 98 crashes. I will tell the story to the best of my memory. Please remember that as of today, this is all hypothetical but will absolutely take place soon.

The setting seemed to be a small Charismatic Church that was engaged in a night singing service. There was a piano, several guitars, and an electric bass. There were about 8-10 people in the choir, the preacher, and another man seated behind the pulpit. The choir director was down on the main floor, pacing back and forth as he led the singing. The camera scanned the congregation, and there seemed to be about 60-75 people of all ages, including infants, small children, and teenagers.

If my memory serves me correctly, the song that they were singing, repeatedly, in typical Pentecostal fashion, was "When We All Get to Heaven." This singing kept going over and over again, with a lot of hand-clapping, for a good 10 minutes or more. All of a sudden, there was an extremely loud noise like standing ten feet behind a big jet plane taking off. Simultaneously there was a flash of light much brighter than the noonday sun. When the rumbling subsided, the brightness began to wane, and it was possible to see that something miraculous and terrifying had taken place.

When normal lighting was restored in the sanctuary, over half of the congregation was gone. The preacher was still there; the choir director was gone. The other man that had been on the platform with the preacher was gone, and all the small children and infants; all gone. Mothers began to scream and wail because they were left holding swaddling clothes and blankets. Some of their husbands were gone. Their babies and husbands had just disappeared. Most of the teenagers in the congregation were still there. No one knew what to say because no one understood what had just taken place.

Realizing that this story is only hypothetical today, we need to ask ourselves, what if this story takes place tomorrow or next week or maybe next year. Will you be one of those left behind, or will you be taken up to heaven to be with our Lord and Savior Jesus Christ. The decision is yours, and only you can make that decision. Just remember that not deciding and accepting Christ as your Savior will condemn you to eternal Hell that the Bible describes as a place of extreme suffering and pain for all of eternity. Perhaps you do not understand just how long eternity is; our finite human minds have trouble understanding such things.

Think of it this way. Scientists tell us that the dinosaurs roamed the earth roughly 40,000,000 to 80,000,000 years ago. The Bible tells us that eternity past was way before that. Think about how much we do not know because the Bible is silent on that subject. Now project out into the future another 80,000,000 years. The Bible tells us that time will only have just begun.

Are you still having trouble deciding for Christ? Go back

and carefully study the pages, WHAT THE BIBLE HAS TO SAY ABOUT HELL. Take the time to look up each scripture in the Bible and read each one. If you think this is too time-consuming, ask yourself this simple question, "how long will I be in the grave? Studying what the Bible has to say about Hell could be the most crucial time you will ever spend in this lifetime.

AFTERWORD

THE NIGHT SALVATION CAME TO CLYDE

*"So shall my word be that goeth forth out of my mouth:
it shall not return unto me void, but it shall
accomplish that which I please, and it shall prosper
in the thing whereto I sent it." Isaiah 55:11*

Many years ago, when I was growing up in Jackson, Mississippi. My family attended Southside Baptist Church at 652 S. Congress Street. It was in this church that I was saved and accepted Jesus Christ as my savior when I was 11 years old, 68years ago.

Recently while reading the Bible, I came across the above scripture. It reminded me of a miracle of sorts that I witnessed one Sunday night during our regular Sunday night service.

First, a little background, there was a very devout family in the church. Tom a deacon, his wife, Francis, and their son Charles. Charles was my age. We were in Sunday school and Training Union together and somewhat friends. Tom had a brother who was the town drunk. His name was Clyde. He and his wife lived about 1.5 blocks from the church in a run-down shack they rented for $15.00 per month. Clyde hadn't held a steady job in years because of his drinking. Most of his clothes and those of his wife came from the Salvation Army. The most he was capable of was doing odd jobs for a few hours at a time. His wife worked as a maid in a dive hotel that paid their bills because Clyde's earnings went for cigarettes and beer.

The miracle. On this Sunday night, the preacher had finished his sermon and given an altar call. For some reason, we did not understand at the time; he kept the choir singing over and over. It went on for perhaps 20 minutes or more. Unbeknownst to those of us in the congregation, the preacher had turned on the huge speakers mounted on the roof of the church. Then, he had the piano and organ stop playing and had the choir switch to a new song, "Just as I am without one plea." We sang that song for several minutes. Over and over, again and again.

Then something strange happened. The back door of the church burst open, and Clyde came running down the aisle. He literally fell flat on his face before the altar and cried uncontrollably, confessing his sins and begging for God's forgiveness. Tom, Francis, and Charles went to the front to be with Clyde. At this point, I doubt that there was a dry eye in the congregation. Everyone in the Church knew how hard Tom had tried to bring his brother to Christ. The odd thing was that even though Clyde still reeked of cigarette smoke and beer, he was sober as if he had never had a drink in his life. Clyde told the church that he had been in the barroom since about 2:00 pm drinking one beer after another. He said that he was blind drunk but somehow had heard the words, "Just as I Am without One Plea" and then "Softly and Tenderly Jesus Is Calling" with the words "O sinner, come home" in the refrain. Clyde said that for whatever reason, he knew those words were meant for him, and this was his last chance. He said that he got up so fast that he knocked over the barstool and ran out the door leaving a few dollars on the bar. He said that he started out walking and then began to run, all the way to the church a block and a half away. Clyde was saved that night and was baptized the next Sunday morning.

Now, for the rest of the story. Clyde had not held a regular job in over 20 years. The following Monday morning, our church custodian turned in his resignation because he had a job offer from a much larger church.

That same night was the monthly deacon's meeting. They voted unanimously to offer the job to Clyde. He accepted, and from that day forward, he was in church every single day of his life until he went to be with the Lord.

To me, this proves Isaiah 55:11 to be true and thinking back, I was privileged to be a witness to this miracle of God.

**The names have been changed to maintain privacy.

Two hymns come to mind as I sit here and write a conclusion to these letters, both taken from The United Methodist Hymn Book. They are "Softly and Tenderly Jesus Is Calling" and "Just As I Am Without One Plea"

Some of the words to the first song:

1. Softly and tenderly, Jesus is calling, calling for you and for me; see, on portals he's waiting and watching, watching for you and for me.

(Refrain)

Come home, come home; ye who are weary come home; earnestly, tenderly, Jesus is calling, calling, O sinner, come home.

2. Why should we tarry when Jesus is pleading, pleading for you and for me? Why should we linger and heed not his mercies, mercies for you and for me?

(Refrain)

3. Time is now fleeting, the moments are passing, passing from you and from me; shadows are gathering, deathbeds are coming, coming for you and for me.

(Refrain)

4. O for the wonderful love he has promised; promised for you and for me! Though we have sinned he has mercy and pardon, pardon for you and for me.

(Refrain)

This was the song the Church was singing the Sunday that I accepted Christ as my Savior and the same one about two years later when my Dad accepted the Lord as his Savior.

The words to the second song that we were singing that night: "Just as I Am Without One Plea," also taken from The United Methodist Hymn Book.

1. Just as I am, without one plea, but that thy blood was shed for me, and that thou bidst me come to thee, O Lamb of God, I come I come.

2. Just as I am and waiting not to rid my soul of one dark blot, to thee whose blood can cleanse each spot, O Lamb of God, I come I come.

3. Just as I am, though tossed about with many a conflict, many a doubt, fighting's and fears within 'and without, O Lamb of God, I come I come

4. Just as I am, poor, wretched, blind; sight, riches, healing of the mind, yea, all I need in thee to find, O Lamb of God, I come I come.

5. Just as I am, thou wilt receive, wilt welcome, pardon, cleanse, relieve; because thy promise I believe, O Lamb of God, I come I come.

6. Just as I am, thy love unknown hath broken every

barrier down; now, to be thine, yea thine alone, O Lamb of God, I come I come.

In closing, let me use the words from a song by Stuart Hamblin, who was a successful Hollywood writer of songs and screenplays. Stuart's father had been a Methodist minister, and he had been raised in the church. Still, that old demon alcohol took hold of him, and he became an alcoholic. This particular night he was blind drunk and was thrown out of the bar. He began stumbling, staggering, and crawling down the street. He found himself sitting up against a building. It was not just any building; it was a small "store-front" Pentecostal church. Stuart sat there and listened for quite a while. He heard the sermon, the altar call, and the singing began; "Just as I am without one plea," etc. Stuart Hamblin had heard enough because God was calling to him. He accepted Christ as his savior that very night, leaning against the side of a building for support, and lived the rest of his life as a Christian. Shortly after that, he wrote the following song:

"It is no secret what God can do; What He's done for others He'll do for you."

Perhaps you can identify with one of the letters and see a need for Jesus in your life; maybe you realize a need today to decide for all of eternity. It is quite easy, just pray a simple prayer, and Jesus will do the rest:

Dear Lord, I want to confess my sins and repent of my sins right now. I am asking for your forgiveness and for you to come into my heart today, at this very moment. I accept you as my Lord and Savior. Amen!

ACKNOWLEDGMENTS

First – I would like to thank my dear wife, Ellen, for tolerating my many hours of confinement in the office while writing and re-writing. She kept reminding me that I had been sitting too long and needed to get up and move around.

Second – Dr. Roberta Wallace for her spiritual guidance and encouragement. Almost every week, I would take her the latest chapters to check for scriptural accuracy where applicable and make corrections as necessary. Without her help, I do not think I could have completed this work.

Third – my mother, Verda "Bert" Landrum Whitehead, 1903 – 1987. She was a remarkable woman, having been born in the piney woods down in south Mississippi in one of the poorest parts of the state. Her father became disabled when she was about 14. Along with her two sisters and her brother, they had to drop out of school and go to work to help keep the family together. They worked for a railroad cutting crossties using crosscut saws—a saw about 10-feet long with a handle on each end requiring two people to operate. On a good day, each pair could cut about five cross-ties. Together they were paid $0.35

for each tie cut or about $5.25 for the day, but they kept the family together.

Mom married dad just before the great depression set in. They made it through those hard times on a farm, living quite well with no shortages of food, which they grew. In 1935, they left the farm and moved to Laurel, MS, where she bought a small neighborhood grocery store, which she kept throughout the war years. Then in August 1942, they adopted me shortly after I was born.

In 1952 we moved to Jackson, MS. The next year she went to work as head housekeeper for a large hotel downtown.

Having been raised as a devout Baptist, the following year, my mother enrolled in a continuing education program in a local Baptist college, Mississippi College.

In 1970 she graduated with a master's degree in Theology, quite an accomplishment for someone with only a 4th or 5th-grade education

ABOUT THE AUTHOR

Raised in Jackson, MS, Tony Whitehead received a music scholarship to the University of Alabama, ROLL TIDE, where he and his wife married and raised two sons. After a short career in law enforcement, Tony started a very successful business before relocating to Baton Rouge, LA, until 1986, when he relocated to the Atlanta, GA area and continued in sales until his retirement in 2016.

Sometime in 2018, after hearing a preacher talking about knowing people who had passed away and probably gone to hell and everlasting torment, the author began thinking about some of the people he had known as a law enforcement officer or classmate and neighbor over the years. This inspired him to confer with his mentor Dr. Roberta Wallace and share the stories in this his first book—*Letters From Hell*.